Design Guerrilla Guide to Typography + InDesign

Mike Pace

Design Guerrilla Guide to Typography + InDesign
© 2025 Mike Pace
All rights reserved. This book or any portion thereof may not be reproduced or used in any manner whatsoever without the express written permission of the publisher except for the use of brief quotations in a book review.
Print ISBN: 979–8–218–80622–4

Contents

Introduction. 5

Before you begin. 6
    Design Philosophy. 7
    Getting Started 8
    Before You Begin: Set Global Preferences. 9
    How This Document Could Be Set Up. 10
    Parent Pages. 11
    Paragraph and Character Styles. 11

Making Styles. 12
Paragraph Styles. 12
    How many paragraph styles should you have? . . 13
    More Style Options 14
    Rules and Shading 14
    Text Inset or Text Indent 16
    Text Alignment 16
    Align to the Baseline Grid 19
    Spanning and Splitting Columns. 19
    Drop Caps and Nested Styles 21
    Bullets and Numbering. 24
    Tabs 25
    Keep Options 26
    Table of Contents (TOC) 27
Character Styles 28
    Small Caps 29
Object Styles 30

Document Structure & Page Anatomy 33
Anatomy of a Page 34
Typography Is Made Consistent With Styles 36
    Auto Style and Style Packs 41

Tables. 44
    Stroke Options 44
    Color 45
    Alignment Within Cells 46
    Text Styles in Tables 46
    Column Spacing 46
    "Exactly" or "At Least" Settings 46
    Anchored Objects and Graphic Cells 47
    Table Headers & Footers 48
    Adjusting Tables 49

Data Merge 50
    Steps for Merging Data 52
    Limitations for Data Merge. 53

Long Documents and InDesign Books 54
    Some Guidelines for Constructing
    Flexible Long Documents 54

GREP 57
    Get a GREP 58
    Some Useful GREP Strings 59
    Finding Text Within Quotation Marks 60
    Find and Change Phone Numbers. 61
    To Find 'between'. 61
    Modify the Search 62
    Save the GREP String 63

Some Useful Tips. 64
    Quick Apply 64
    Footnotes and Endnotes 64
    Glyphs and Special Characters 65
    Shaping Text Frames. 66
    Alternate Layouts and Liquid Layout Rules. . . . 67
    Jump Lines. 68
    Story Editor and Copy Editor. 69
    Linking and Duplicating Content. 70
    Copying and Applying Text or Object Attributes . 70
    Fitting Objects to Frames. 71

Interactive Documents 73
    Hyperlinks 73
    Buttons. 76
    Slideshows. 77

Considerations for Digital and Print Output. 80
    Starting With Spreads 80
    Color Spaces, Graphic Formats and Resolution . . 80
    Process and Spot Colors 82
    About Ink Trapping 82
    Gradients and Gradient Feather. 84
    Adding Color to Grayscale Images 84
    Single Pages and Spreads 85
    Print Booklet and Booklet Types 87
    Imposition 88
    Preflighting, Output and Packaging 91

So Wait… What Is Typography? 93
    Character Anatomy 93
    Glossary of Type Anatomy 94
    A Very, Very Brief History of Western Type. 95

Crimes Against Typography. 106

g

Mike Pace, professor emeritus of visual design, ex surfer, cyclist and part-time randonneur, is an award-winning photographer and designer living in the most north-eastern neighborhood of Los Angeles. When not restituting crimes against typography, he is probably looking for zen-in-now moments and thinking not very deep thoughts.

Design Guerrilla: *An ethical rebel fighting against the visual tyranny of mediocrity in design and typography, especially where crimes against typography occur. One who employs fluid, instinctual and at times disruptive techniques.*

IF a designer is like a surfer riding the waves of design, leaving exhilarating trails of ephemeral calligraphy inscribed across fluid faces, is it more thrilling to surf naked? This question isn't answered here, but you'll find practical tips to streamline and enhance your InDesign practices. After all, great design is based on iteration after iteration after iteration.

Culminating decades of design and teaching, this guide distills those interactions and observations into a compendium of the most common techniques used to create eye-catching and powerful typography-oriented design, techniques unfettered from particular application versions. This is not a user manual covering every tool or arcane usage; there are numerous in-app and online help guides for that. Rather, it is an in-depth practical guide for the most useful and important InDesign typography practices, hopefully enabling you to streamline your process, taking your design from ordinary to extraordinary.

Although at times experimental, pushing against the elastic bounds of legibility and readability, the content within these pages tries to avoid Crimes Against Typography and scrutiny from the ever-perspicacious Department of Typography Police. While the interplay between typography and design is often enhanced by using an array of design apps, this guide, however, focuses on InDesign, and includes its usage of generative AI to develop some of the graphic content.

—Mike Pace, September 2025

Guide to Typography + InDesign | 5

Before you begin...

¶ PAGE LAYOUT APPLICATIONS ARE TOOLS FOR PRODUCTION. They are intended to work with text-heavy documents, but can be used for picture books—in fact, any document more than a couple of pages long is best suited to a page layout application. Illustrator and Photoshop can of course be used, but they are much more time consuming and cumbersome to use for multi-page documents. Effective designers use the best tool, or application, for the job.

Essentially, page design is about the flow of text with images. It is primarily concerned with typography, not image manipulation, and the relationship between type and image. It achieves its design goals by providing consistency and the ability to later easily edit changes.

It is assumed you are already familiar with opening or creating documents, flowing text, and linking text frames. So, to begin, here are terms and concepts you need to be familiar with:

- **Styles**: These allow you to consistently format text by paragraph (globally for the whole document, or by individual paragraphs) or by character (locally, for individual characters or words within a paragraph). They are essential for consistent design. Note: a paragraph is created every time the return key is hit, so paragraphs can be empty. Graphic elements, objects, can also be styled
- **Parent Pages**: The skeletal grid structures that underpin the document when you first create it. They are initially formed by the margin and column settings. You can subsequently create multiple Parent pages, independent of each other, for different layouts or sections in your document. An essential attribute of Parent pages is their ability to contain repeating elements, like page numbers or running heads. Simply, any element on a Parent page will be displayed on all pages in the document that use that Parent.
- **Typography**: The art and design of type and text, based on its ability to clearly communicate its intended message and to do so in a visually effective way.
- **Fonts**: Type is the backbone of design. Font families often have different variations or 'faces' associated with them, for example, Regular, *Italic*, and **Bold**. These variations are not computer generated, but are actual designed typefaces. Some families are extensive and include additional variations like Light, Condensed, Extended, and **Black**. The 'Pro' versions of type families are typically the ones with more faces.
- **Glyphs**: Many fonts also include alternate characters, ligatures (specially designed fonts for combinations of the letters f, l, j and i—ff, ffl, ffi, ffj, fj, fl, fi), swashes (ornate calligraphic lines ⌒, ⌒, ⌒) and ornaments (❋, ❋, ❦). These can be accessed via the Glyphs panel. Not all fonts will have glyph sets.

- **Leading**: Type sits on a baseline, and leading (pronounced *ledding*) is the space between baselines. You should never use 'Auto' leading for line spacing. Always set a number. If unsure, begin with 2 points more than the type size, and adjust in increments of 2 points. Well-set type is better created optically than by following numbers, especially since different fonts families at the same size will often appear to be bigger or smaller in relation to each other.
- **Tracking and Kerning**: These terms refer to the spacing between words (tracking) and between letters (kerning). Paragraphs are often tracked to compose them better into the space they occupy. Words, especially at larger type sizes, are often kerned to adjust the spacing between characters for a better optical fit.
- **Baseline Grid**: A *Preferences* setting that you can force your text to snap to. If snapping to the grid, it should be equal to your leading or a multiple of it. Its visibility is turned off by default.
- **Hidden or Invisible Characters**: These are non-printing visual indicators that represent things like spaces (between words or letters), tabs, paragraphs (whenever the 'return' key is hit) etc. It is very useful to have them turned on (off by default):

¶ indicates paragraph breaks | ¬ indicates line breaks | » indicates tab spaces | · indicates spaces

Design Philosophy

¶ Always assume you will have to edit your design, often extensively, at a later stage. To this end, correctly named and applied styles can make your design process more efficient. You won't have to reinvent the wheel every time you want to make a typographic change down the line. Especially when your original intent might be a dim and cluttered memory (yes, you think you'll remember the finer details and differences between Paragraph Style 7 and Paragraph Style 3, but you won't).

In InDesign, Character Styles will always override Paragraph Styles. This means that sometimes when you apply a paragraph style either nothing happens or something unexpected happens because a character style might inadvertently be dominating the paragraph style's settings. Bearing this in mind, consider *not* using *leading* as a character attribute. Rather set it as a paragraph attribute. Some guidelines:

- If the styling applies to anything that ends with a line break, whether a word or paragraph, use Paragraph Styles.
- If you have to select something within a paragraph to change its style, like a word or bunch of words, use Character Styles.
- Never use auto-leading for your paragraphs: always assign a fixed value, 2 to 4 pts greater than your text size, for readability (the text in this document is 10/14: 10 pt type with 14 pt leading).
- Base your Document and Baseline grids on your leading.
- Apply leading to whole paragraphs.

- If you use a different leading value for headings and larger display-type sizes, use a leading that is a multiple of your base leading to keep line spacing consistent (for this document that would be a 28 pt leading for larger type sizes—2 x 14).
- Snap your text to your based-on-leading Baseline grid, especially if you have text in side-by-side columns. It will then always be aligned across columns.
- If you want to reuse your styles and have easy access to them in other documents, save them to your CC Libraries.
- Generally use as few text frames as possible. If you can, keep all your text in a single frame, or in linked/threaded text frames. Be Zen: text is a stream you want to keep flowing smoothly.

Getting Started

¶ When InDesign opens, it opens in the Essentials workspace. Change this to Advanced in the pull-down menu at the top right of the Applications Bar for a more comprehensive workspace. You may choose other preset workspaces from it, or create your own. The Application Frame runs across the top of the screen in all workspaces. The Control Bar, which spans the screen under the Application Frame, is interactive and changes in accordance to the tools selected in the Tools panel and the workspace chosen. The amount of information displayed in the Options bar is dependent on monitor/screen resolution. The Context Bar displays information based on where the cursor is placed. Note, the appearance of the InDesign interface shown in this document has been changed from the default Dark color theme to Medium Light, found under the Interface tab in the *Preferences* panel.

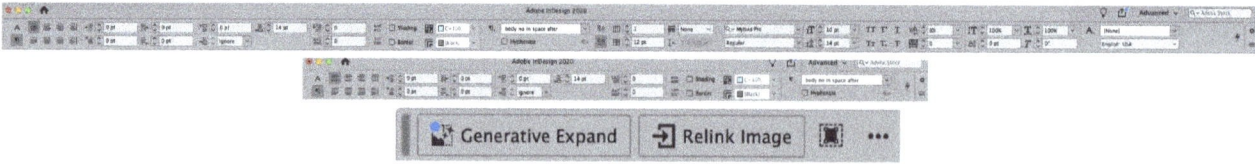

Page layout works on a user-defined grid system that begins with the creation of a new document. The skeletal grid structure of the document is called a Parent Page, and you can have as many Parent pages as you need to organize your layout. Generally, your document setup (when you create a new document) matches the same specifications as a single page, not a spread, of what you will be creating. In InDesign additional grids are created by setting up the Document Grid (which looks like graph paper and can be as simple or complex as you need) and the Baseline Grid (which looks like ruled paper and should be based on leading). Guides can also be dragged off the Rulers for further customization. Grids are essential for the arrangement of type and graphics, and it is useful to base them on the typographic structure used in the document.

Styles are used to consistently format blocks of text, and are really useful for updating text that occurs in multiple places across a document. For text there are two types of Styles to consider: Character and Paragraph. The overall or global look of a document is affected by Paragraph Styles, while individual characters or words may be locally formatted with Character Styles. Good design practice takes into consideration the inevitability of editing or making changes that need to occur later (often *after* you think a job is done). Styles make light work of the drudge of having to recreate or change typographic elements. They are easy to create and you should get in the habit of always using them. Object Styles are essentially used for consistent frame and line elements. They can also specify paragraph styles within text frames.

Typographic elements include type family (Garamond, Helvetica, etc.) and face (**Bold**, *Italic*, Regular, etc.); size (in points); leading (the space between lines, also in points); alignment (right, left, centered, or justified); tracking and kerning (the space between words and letters); and hyphenation (how and if words break). Do not lose control of your type, especially its line spacing—again, *never* user 'Auto' leading. Always specify what leading you wish to use.

To customize the way you want InDesign to work, set the Application Preferences before you open or create a new document. If, for example, you always want to start with a specific font, size, and leading (as opposed to the default setting with auto-leading), you can set these globally so that every new document you create will begin this way. You can even include type and object styles, customized colors, and grids.

Before You Begin: Set Global Preferences

OPEN INDESIGN BUT DO NOT OPEN OR **create a new document.** Click on the Type Tool in the Tools panel. Select the Character Formatting Controls in the Control bar at the top of the screen, choose the typeface you want to use as your default, then set its point size *and* its leading:

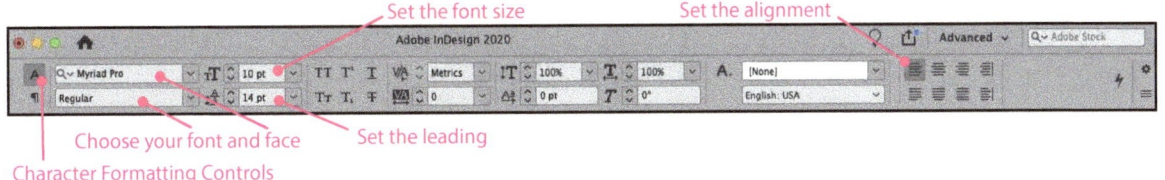

Other preferences to set are found in Preferences (cmd+K) under the InDesign menu (Edit menu on PC: ctrl+K) at the top of the screen.

- To help snapping text to the baseline grid, in the Grids option set the increment for the *Baseline Grid* to match your leading, starting at 0 pt relative to the top of page. For the *Document Grid* multiply your leading by 10 and make this your Gridline increment, and enter 10 as the number for subdivisions. Why 10? Arithmetic may not be your friend and multiplying by 10 is easy. Remember to reset the baseline and document grid increments whenever you change your document's base leading.
- *Enable Drag and Drop Text Editing* in the Type option. Enabling *Smart Text Reflow* (end of story) allows InDesign to automatically add new

pages for you. This is very useful when placing text. You can also choose to have empty pages deleted.

- Set the Character Settings for *Small Caps* in the Advanced Type option to around 70% – 75% to prevent SMALL CAPS from appearing too skinny. This should always be changed in relation to the fonts used.
- The default setting for the Ruler increments is in points. You can change this in the Units and Increments option to inches or centimeters or any other measurement system you prefer. You can also change these on the fly within the document by *right-clicking* on both the horizontal and vertical rulers to access the contextual pull-down menu associated with them, and selecting the measurement option you want to use.

A note about measurements: Some of the input fields are measurement-system sensitive. Fields associated with indents, spacing and dimensions, for example, reflect the measurement system chosen in the rulers. You can, however, input data in any measurement system you wish and InDesign will convert it for you. For example, your document uses inches, and you want to specify a first-line indent of 10 points, you simply type '10 pt' (or 'p10') into the appropriate input box and InDesign will do the conversion for you. You need type to be a specific size that is not in points? Type '6 cm' or '2.25 in' or whatever size needs to be specified into the Font Size box and InDesign will take care of it.

You can also set up your own set of global styles for text and graphics. Once you have settled on styles that you use consistently, you can import those styles from other InDesign documents, if they have been used there (they don't have to be open), by using the Load Styles command found in the pull-down menu in the *Paragraph Styles* panel. Similarly, colors can also be appended by using the Load Swatches command in the pull-down of the *Swatches* panel. Remember, loading styles and colors into InDesign, without an open document makes those styles global, that is, they will be embedded into every new document you create. Doing so to an existing open document makes them part of the open document only.

How This Document Could Be Set Up

A single page document with a centered text frame is created by unchecking the Facing Pages check box. Its dimensions are as follows:

- 3:4 aspect ratio, 594 pt x 792 pt (8.25 in x 11 in)
- Top margin is 38 pt (0.5278 in)
- Bottom margin is 54 pt (0.75 in)
- Left margin is 134 pt (1.889 in)
- Right margin is 134 pt (1.889 in)

After the document is created additional Parent Pages are setup for text with a sidebar for graphical or explanatory content. Page numbers and repeating elements are added to *all* Parent Pages at this point.

- Left margin is set to 214 pt (2.9722 in)
- Top, bottom and right margins are set to 54 pt
- Guides are positioned to facilitate consistent layout

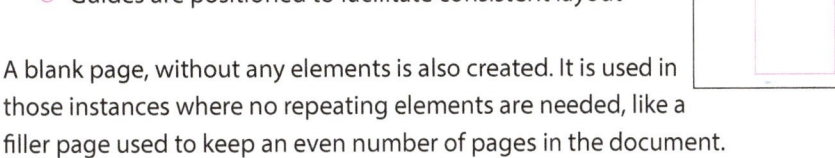

A blank page, without any elements is also created. It is used in those instances where no repeating elements are needed, like a filler page used to keep an even number of pages in the document.

Parent Pages

A PARENT PAGE IS ALWAYS CREATED WHEN the document is first set up (it will be found in the top section of the Pages panel). It is called *A-Parent* by default. It helps to change the names of the Parent pages you create to make them more easily identifiable. Consistency is maintained by placing repeating elements on the Parents. In this document page numbering, a running footer, and a logotype identifier are used. These all appear on the Parent pages used for different page sections.

Paragraph and Character Styles

NAME STYLES IN A WAY THAT MAKE sense to you. For example, in this document's styles *"no in"* indicates that there is no first line indent in the paragraph style. This style is typically used under a sub heading. The *"body no in space after"* style implies body text with no first line indent and automatic spacing between paragraphs (the space after the paragraph is equal to the leading to maintain consistent spacing).

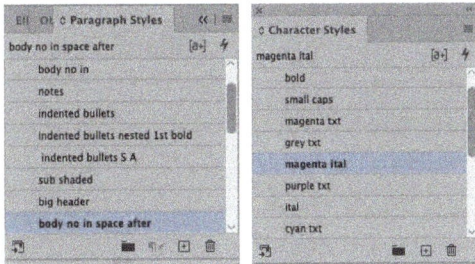

All differently formatted text within paragraphs, like the italicized magenta-colored text on this page, is a locally applied character style, *"magenta ital."* The small caps at the beginning of the opening paragraph are a character style nested within a paragraph style.

Making Styles

Paragraph Styles

¶ You don't need to select a paragraph in order to apply a style to it: as long as the Text tool cursor is anywhere within a paragraph, clicking a paragraph style name in the Paragraph Styles panel will apply that style to it. Don't have any styles created? No problem. Put your cursor anywhere in the paragraph, then open the Paragraph Styles panel and choose New Paragraph Style from the top right pull-down menu, or by clicking the little + on the bottom right of the panel. Having the cursor in the paragraph allows you to see any typographic changes you make in real time, if you have the Apply Style to Selection and Preview boxes checked in the General sub-panel.

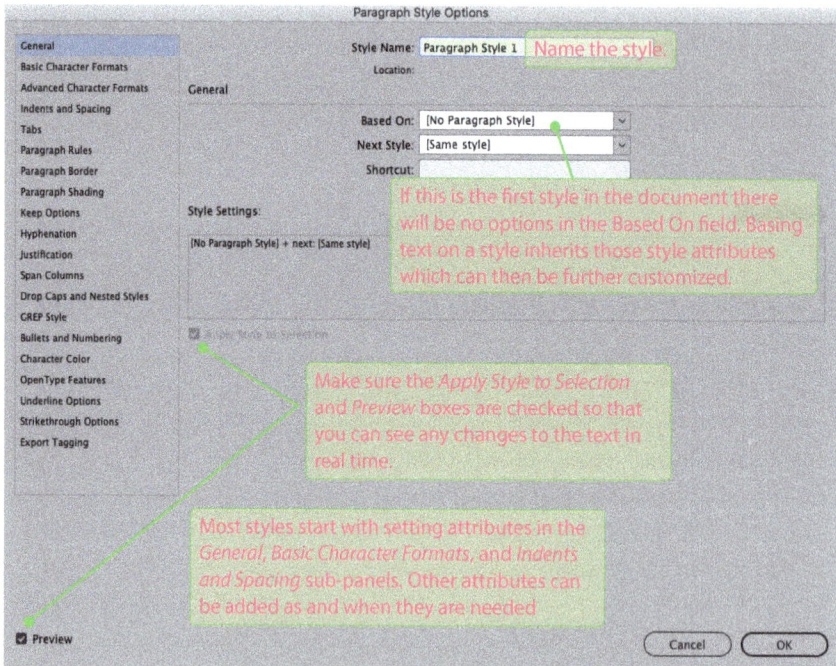

You can also import styles from another InDesign document (Load Paragraph Styles… in the same Paragraph Styles pull-down menu). Don't have text? Still no problem, drag a text frame with the Text tool and fill it with placeholder text (Type –> Fill With Placeholder Text), then open the Paragraph Styles panel and make a new style. Name this style in a way that is meaningful. Note: clicking to apply a style only works with character styles if you have something selected.

The next sub-panel to open is Basic Character Formats to set the typeface, size and leading attributes, followed by Indents and Spacing. (These panels are shown on the next page). Any other changes, things like hyphenation settings, tabs, rules (i.e. lines), alternate stylings etc., can be added later or based off these settings.

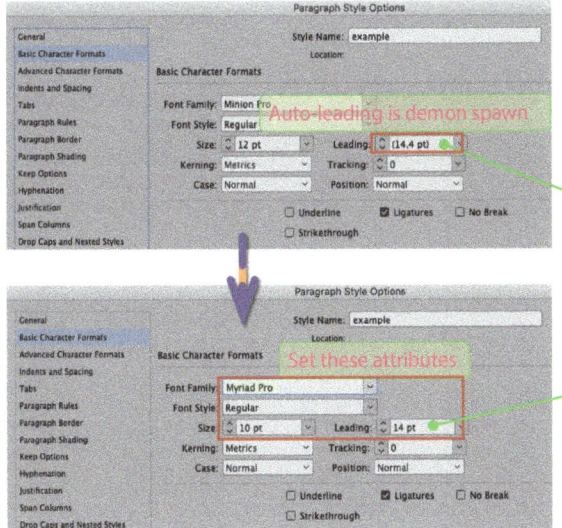

After setting the General preferences, set the *Basic Character Formats*. This is where you set the Font Family (like Myriad Pro) and Style (like Regular), its Size and Leading. Note that a leading value inside brackets (14.4 pt) indicates that auto-leading is used because no leading value has been set. Auto-leading in InDesign defaults at 120% of the type size.

Remember, your leading values should match your baseline grid for snapping to be effective.

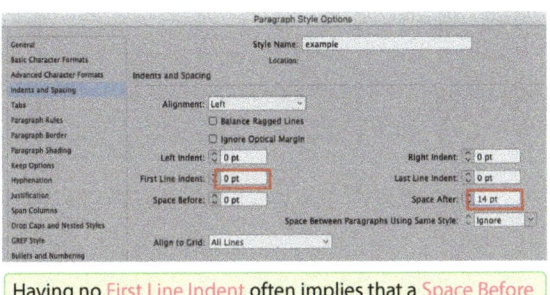

The next attributes to be set are found in the *Indents and Spacing* sub-panel. Business style block paragraphs use spaces between paragraphs for separation.
Long documents, like stories or articles, generally use First Line Indents to visually separate paragraphs from each other.

Having no *First Line Indent* often implies that a *Space Before* or *After* will be applied to separate the paragraphs.

One benefit of using styles is that it makes updating or changing any type attributes really easy. Instead of having to select bunches of paragraphs to make changes, simply make the change to the style and every instance of the style will be updated. You can either make the change in Paragraph Styles menu, or in the text itself and then choose *Redefine Style* from the Paragraph Styles pull-down menu to incorporate those changes back into the style. Or save it as a *new* style if you want to keep both variations.

How many paragraph styles should you have?

THE NUMBER OF STYLES YOU USE WILL usually be determined by the type of document you are formatting. You will need at least one style for your body text. If your design uses a flush left section-opening paragraph followed by first line indented paragraphs then you would have a style for each of those. If you use headings and subheadings, you'll have styles for those too. Basically, any formatting that will be reused should be saved as a style.

Consider setting any styles that you consistently use as global styles for your document: after opening InDesign but before opening a document you can *Load All Styles* from documents that use the styles you want. This will then allow you to have your most used styles always available in any new document. To change the formatting for any new project that requires it, simply change the style attributes.

More Style Options

This is an overview of some fancy and not-so-fancy things you can do with in the Paragraph Styles.

Rules and Shading

This is a paragraph rule   ◂ This is a 0.5 pt Rule Below. Rules are measured from the baseline.

This is also a paragraph rule   ◂ This is a 14 pt Rule Above, -4 pt left and right indents, -4 pt offset.

This uses two paragraph rules   ◂ 14 pt Rule Above, with a 2 pt Rule Below and -8 pt left indent

These rules have their width set to Text. Indents are used to modify their lengths in relation to the text. You can make paragraph rules in the Paragraph Styles panel, or from the pull-down menu on the Paragraphs panel. Since rules (lines) lie behind text, they can be used to "highlight" by adjusting their thickness, and offset amount which raises or lowers them from the baseline.

This is paragraph shading   ◂ Paragraph Shading, with a 2 pt offset

This is also paragraph shading, with a border and a rule   ◂ Paragraph Shading, with 2 pt rounded corners for border and shading, and 2 pt offset

This is also paragraph shading. With a border and a rule. The "highlight" is a rule. This paragraph is not a separate text frame but part of the text flow. It uses indents to shift it from the left and right margins.

Paragraph Borders and Shading… (Paragraph panel) or the *Paragraph Border* and *Paragraph Shading* sub panels in Paragraph Styles allow for adjustments including corner size, shape and offset.

This paragraph is shaded blue and has a paragraph border, which is offset from the edge of the shading. This paragraph and the one below are in the same text frame. The paragraphs are *not* indented from the large frame surrounding them.

All the text in this frame, i.e these two shaded paragraphs, is *inset* away from the edges of the *text frame* by 10 pts, Object –> Text Frame Options –> Inset Spacing. The rounded corner radius is also 10 pts. This frame has its own fill color (light yellow) and border. The border stroke is 4 pt Thin-Thin (orange) with Gap Color enabled (yellow). It is an attribute of the primary text frame.

You could draw lines and use frames behind text to get similar effects, but styles give you consistency, and more importantly, they adjust and flow with the text during editing since they are part of the text. In the rare cases where you can't achieve your effect with styles or built-in attributes, then by all means resort to drawing lines and frames.

> Rather than a colored box (rotated and moved up here) behind colored type, it's preferable to use Paragraph Shading.

A Subheading ¶

This is the *body no in style*. It begins flush left, has *no indent*, and runs ragged. It is typically used as the beginning paragraph below a heading style. Name your styles so that you, or others if you are in a workgroup, can easily identify them. ¶

Another Subheading ¶

> ► This is an indented bullets style with no space after the paragraph, resulting in closely spaced bullets¶
> ► pro conectur lorum ipsum¶
> ► id ma doloris sit ¶

> The text in this example is formatted with too many frames. Note the thin blue borders that indicate the text frames. Compare to the bottom example which is just a single frame, with paragraph formatting applied.
>
> The ¶ symbol was added to the end of paragraphs to indicate line breaks (as if you were viewing Hidden Characters).

A Heading ¶

A Subheading ¶

This is the *body no in style*. It begins flush left, has *no indent*, and runs ragged. It is typically used as the beginning paragraph below a heading style. Name your styles so that you, or others if you are in a workgroup, can easily identify them. ¶

Another Subheading ¶

► This is an indented bullets style with no space after the paragraph, resulting in closely spaced bullets¶
► pro conectur lorum ipsum¶
► id ma doloris sit ¶

> Below is the unformatted text used for this example.
>
> A Heading ¶
> A Subheading ¶
> This is the body no in style. It begins flush left, has no indent, and runs ragged. It is typically used as the beginning paragraph below a heading style. Name your styles so that you, or others if you are in a workgroup, can easily identify them. ¶
> Another Subheading ¶
> This is an indented bullets style with no space after the paragraph, resulting in closely spaced bullets ¶
> pro conectur lorum ipsum¶
> id ma doloris sit ¶

Text Inset or Text Indent

So what is the difference? Think of *insets* as padding in a text frame, a space that you create to buffer the text from the edge of the frame. They can be saved as *object* styles. An *indent* is a paragraph attribute that you can apply to push text away from the frame, and inset, if one is applied. They seem to be similar, so when should you use which?

The 4 pt *inset* matches the corner radius of the frame (Frame attribute). This can be saved as an Object Style.

A Heading

A Subheading

This is the *body no in style*. It begins flush left, has *no indent*, and runs ragged. It is typically used as the beginning paragraph below a heading style. Name your styles so that you, or others if you are in a workgroup, can easily identify them.

Another Subheading

- This is the indented bullets style no space after the paragraph
- pro conectur lorum ipsum
- id ma doloris sit

Indents are used to push the text away from the inset. They can be saved as a Paragraph Style.

The unsightly squishing of the text on the left edge is solved by using a text inset, a text frame attribute (Object –> Text Frame Options –> Inset Spacing). Try a 4 pt inset as a starting point.

InDesign's default text frames do not have insets. This is usually not a problem until you color the background of the text frame.

InDesign's default text frames do not have insets. This is usually not a problem until you color the background of the text frame.

Text Alignment

Alignment: Text is usually Left aligned and runs ragged on the right edge of the paragraph, meaning the right side of a text block is uneven against that edge. This document is set that way. Other alignment options are Centered, Right aligned, and Justified, meaning both edges run flush with the margins. Justified text also has settings for how the last line of the paragraph runs: the last line can be left aligned, centered, right aligned, or justified which means the remaining words are spread across the column or text frame.

The following paragraphs show examples of alignment.

Left aligned: Sedit arunti cus am volorpor aciisqu iature, si aci ut omnis que cum reicat is ariosam fugiat. Ernatis atinvendam qui consequas molenis magnis cus perferum il il imi, volent.

> These are the common paragraph alignments. First line indents may be used with any left aligned paragraphs, including justified ones. Note that when using justified text there will often be tracking issues—the spaces between words often become quite unsightly. The text will need to be manually tracked to avoid those funky gaps.

    Left aligned with a first line indent: Sedit arunti cus am volorpor aciisqu iature, si aci ut omnis que cum reicat is ariosam fugiat. Ernatis atinvendam qui consequas molenis magnis cus perferum il il imi, volent.

Center aligned: Sedit arunti cus am volorpor aciisqu iature, si aci ut omnis que cum reicat is ariosam fugiat. Ernatis atinvendam qui consequas molenis magnis cus perferum il il imi, volent.

Right aligned: Sedit arunti cus am volorpor aciisqu iature, si aci ut omnis que cum reicat is ariosam fugiat. Ernatis atinvendam qui consequas molenis magnis cus perferum il il imi, volent.

Justified with last line left aligned: Sedit arunti cus am volorpor aciisqu iature, si aci ut omnis que cum reicat is ariosam fugiat. Ernatis atinvendam qui consequas molenis magnis cus perferum il il imi, volent.

    Justified with first line indent and last line left aligned: Sedit arunti cus am volorpor aciisqu iature, si aci ut omnis que cum reicat is ariosam fugiat. Ernatis atinvendam qui consequas molenis magnis cus perferum il il imi, volent.

Justified with last line center aligned: Sedit arunti cus am volorpor aciisqu iature, si aci ut omnis que cum reicat is ariosam fugiat. Ernatis atinvendam qui consequas molenis magnis cus perferum il il imi, volent.

Justified with last line right aligned: Sedit arunti cus am volorpor aciisqu iature, si aci ut omnis que cum reicat is ariosam fugiat. Ernatis atinvendam qui consequas molenis magnis cus perferum il il imi, volent.

Justifiy all lines: Sedit arunti cus am volorpor aciisqu iature, si aci ut omnis que cum reicat is ariosam fugiat. Ernatis atinvendam qui consequas molenis magnis cus perferum il il imi, volent.

> Leaving text spaced like this will result in you be harangued by the Department of Typography Police for crimes against typography.

Hanging Indents: Whereas a first line indent has the text following the first line aligned to the left of the text frame, hanging indents have the text following the first line indented away from the left edge of the text frame.

To create hanging indents, indent all the text away from the left frame edge, and then apply that indent as a negative amount to the first line indent:

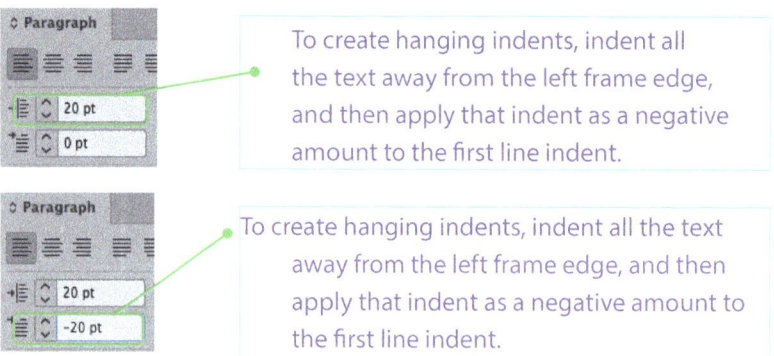

To create hanging indents, indent all the text away from the left frame edge, and then apply that indent as a negative amount to the first line indent.

To create hanging indents, indent all the text away from the left frame edge, and then apply that indent as a negative amount to the first line indent.

Hanging indents are often used with bulleted lists to keep multiple lines of text within the bullet point aligned away from the bullets:

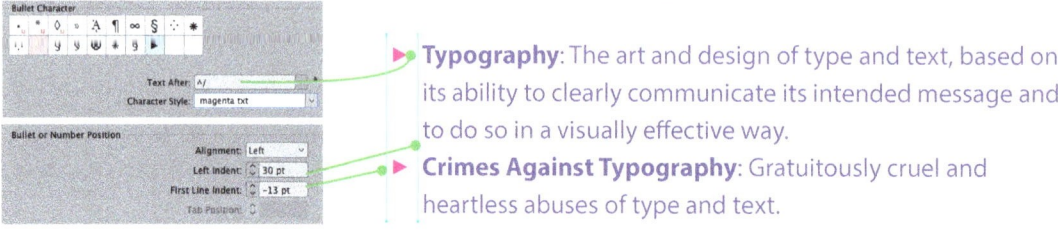

▶ **Typography**: The art and design of type and text, based on its ability to clearly communicate its intended message and to do so in a visually effective way.
▶ **Crimes Against Typography**: Gratuitously cruel and heartless abuses of type and text.

A hanging indent is not used in this example below (first line indent 0 pt):

▶ **Typography**: The art and design of type and text, based on its ability to clearly communicate its intended message and to do so in a visually effective way.
▶ **Crimes Against Typography**: Gratuitously cruel and heartless abuses of type and text.

These are among the spacing options for the text following the bullet (the code symbols are substituted by InDesign after you choose the type of space you want to use):

Choose the spacing between the bullets and text that best fits with your design. The *Text After* pull-down menu also allows for other options including dashes and tabs. You can input multiple options.

▶ **Text after an en space**: ^>
▶ **Text after an em space**: ^m
▶ **Text after a hair space**: ^|
▶ **Text after a thin space**: ^<
▶ **Text after a figure space**: ^/
▶ **Text after a punctuation space**: ^.
▶– **Text after an en dash and punctuation space**: ^=^.

Align to the Baseline Grid

Generally your paragraph styles should align the text to the baseline grid, especially when there are side-by-side columns. Misaligned columns are considered a crime against typography, but are avoided by snapping.

> You may not care about small crimes against typography like the misaligned text in these columns. But the Department of Typography Police does.

Ovidemqu iandemporita cusdandam conseniam, simagnis magnatis disi voluptaqui doluptis arum facietur, quibusae reperib earciam reic temque iur, consequi disquidipsum exped quo. Dundion rehene ommolup tatet, et quasim sam, estiore quas volum

plit, evendunt pa nat ab ium simusda nimusda ercidelecum et, quia quunt iunt excest, et qui sumquunt. Tem et eum verume volentorum voloribea paritio. Itatus duscium vel maiore nosto tem con cullendae venem essus et omniendaecto cum ut andent, poroba

> Snapping to the baseline makes the text more legible, more readable, and will save you from the ire of the Typography Police.

Ovidemqu iandemporita cusdandam conseniam, simagnis magnatis disi voluptaqui doluptis arum facietur, quibusae reperib earciam reic temque iur, consequi disquidipsum exped quo. Dundion rehene ommolup tatet, et quasim

evendunt pa nat ab ium simusda nimusda ercidelecum et, quia quunt iunt excest, et qui sumquunt. Tem et eum verume volentorum voloribea paritio. Itatus duscium vel maiore nosto tem con cullendae venem essus et omniendaecto cum ut

There are exceptions. For example, when using sidebar text that uses a different font size and leading, like the text on the right. ▶
The first line of the text is aligned to the grid.

> The text in this frame does not snap to the grid. It uses 8 pt type on 10 pt leading. If it snapped to the grid it would effectively have a leading of 14 pts.

Spanning and Splitting Columns

Paragraphs span the text frame column width. You can create side by side columns using linked text frames, by subdividing a text frame into columns, or by "splitting" a single text frame.

Splitting divides the selected paragraphs into the number of columns (splits) you designate. Spanning will run selected paragraphs across a designated number of splits or columns. If you subdivide the *frame* into columns (Object –> Text Frame Options…), and not the *page* (Layout –> Margins and Columns…), you can also span paragraphs across them.

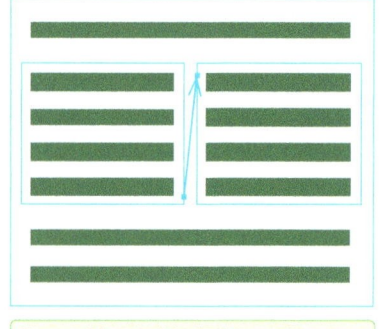

You could probably do this, using multiple text frames and cutting and pasting your text into linked frames…

…but using a paragraph split is a better solution and a time saver.

This paragraph spans the text frame since the text frame is *not* subdivided into columns.

If your document is primarily one column wide, like this one, splitting paragraphs when needed is an efficient way to keep text flowing without resorting to using multiple text frames, especially if the splits are specified as paragraph styles.

This indented text is set to *split* into three columns. Fugiati rem assequi squatempe excero temporum estius qui aut ommolupta volorro id minci re suntibustrum ipissit aspedip itatestius con et vent. Tio. Tas quo mos es rehendi tionsec earchilla quas dolorep ratempore doloribus, sus et aut et earchilla quas dolorep.

This paragraph spans the text frame again. Fugiati rem assequi squatempe excero temporum estius qui aut ommolupta volorro id minci re suntibustrum ipissit aspedip itatestius con et vent.

This text frame is subdivided into *three* columns. This paragraph *spans* the text frame (Span All), overriding the default column subdivisions.

Similarly, multi-column documents benefit from having the text frame subdivided into columns and having spanned paragraphs as styles.

This paragraph's text automatically flows into the three columns. It is not split into three columns. Fugiati rem assequi squatempe excero temporum estius qui aut ommolupta volorro id minci re suntibustrum ipissit aspedip itatestius con et vent. Tio. Tas quo mos es rehendi tionsec earchilla quas dolorep ratempore doloribus, sus et aut et earchilla quas dolorep.

This paragraph spans all the columns again. Fugiati rem assequi squatempe excero temporum estius qui aut ommolupta volorro id minci re suntibustrum ipissit aspedip itatestius con et vent.

Using the Paragraph or Paragraph Styles panel to create the spans and splits allows for many options to be included into the style, like spacing between the splits (gutters), indents from the outside margins, and spacing before or after the paragraphs to separate them out from the rest of the text.

Drop Caps and Nested Styles

Drop caps and initial caps are used to indicate opening section starts or paragraphs in a document, and are not used for consecutive paragraphs. Drop caps are large characters that drop below the first baseline. In InDesign this is specified by a the number of lines you want the character to "drop"—the more lines specified, the larger the character. Initial caps sit on the first baseline and grow upward, their size dependent on the point size specified. Both drop caps and initial caps can be modified by nested styles. Nested styles allow you to attached character styles to a paragraph styles in order to format specific parts of a paragraph.

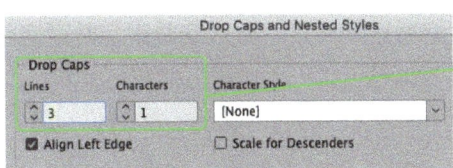

Drop caps are used to indicate opening section starts or paragraphs in a document, and are not used for consecutive paragraphs. Drop caps are large characters that drop below the first baseline. In InDesign this is specified by a the number of lines you want the character to "drop"—the more lines specified, the larger the character.

The default drop cap. No Character Style applied.

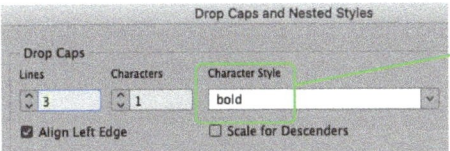

Drop caps are used to indicate opening section starts or paragraphs in a document, and are not used for consecutive paragraphs. Drop caps are large characters that drop below the first baseline. In InDesign this is specified by a the number of lines you want the character to "drop"—the more lines specified, the larger the character.

A "bold" Character Style applied to the drop cap.

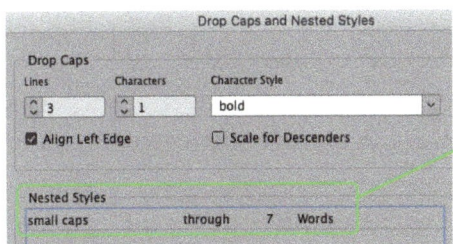

DROP CAPS ARE USED TO INDICATE OPENING section starts or paragraphs in a document, and are not used for consecutive paragraphs. Drop caps are large characters that drop below the first baseline. In InDesign this is specified by a the number of lines you want the character to "drop"—the more lines specified, the larger the character.

Additionally, a "small caps" Nested Character Style applied to the first seven words in the paragraph after the drop cap.

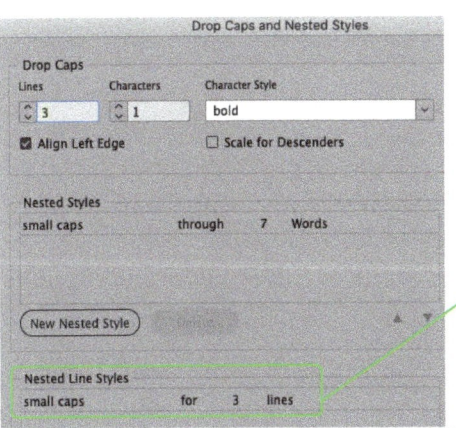

DROP CAPS ARE USED TO INDICATE OPENING SECTION STARTS OR PARAGRAPHS IN A DOCUMENT, AND ARE NOT USED FOR CONSECUTIVE PARAGRAPHS. DROP CAPS ARE LARGE CHARACTERS THAT DROP BELOW the first baseline. In InDesign this is specified by a the number of lines you want the character to "drop"—the more lines specified, the larger the character.

A Line Style continues the nested style for three lines to match the drop cap

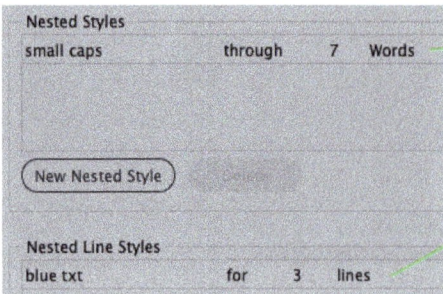

DROP CAPS ARE USED TO INDICATE OPENING section starts or paragraphs in a document, and are not used for consecutive paragraphs. Drop caps are large characters that drop below the first baseline. In InDesign this is specified by a the number of lines you want the character to "drop"—the more lines specified, the larger the character.

The drop cap is a bigger size—14 pt— and so extends above the ascender height of the first line. The size and color can be applied as a character style.

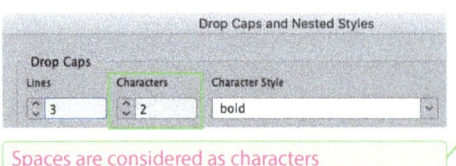

Spaces are considered as characters

DROP CAPS ARE USED TO INDICATE OPENING section starts or paragraphs in a document, and are not used for consecutive paragraphs. Drop caps are large characters that drop below the first baseline. In InDesign this is specified by a the number of lines you want the character to "drop"—the more lines specified, the larger the character.

To pull the drop cap out of the frame to the left, insert a space before it, set the number of characters to be affected to 2, and then put the cursor before the drop cap and kern it negatively until it is in the desired position: press option/alt and tap the left arrow to move the drop cap into the space.

DROP CAPS ARE USED TO INDICATE OPENING section starts or paragraphs in a document, and are not used for consecutive paragraphs. Drop caps are large characters that drop below the first baseline. In InDesign this is specified by a the number of lines you want the character to "drop"—the more lines specified, the larger the character.

DROP CAPS ARE USED TO INDICATE OPENING section starts or paragraphs in a document, and are not used for consecutive paragraphs. Drop caps are large characters that drop below the first baseline. In InDesign this is specified by a the number of lines you want the character to "drop"—the more lines specified, the larger the character.

Drop caps are often in a contrasting typeface. These can also be set as Character Styles.

DROP CAPS ARE USED TO INDICATE OPENING section starts or paragraphs in a document, and are not used for consecutive paragraphs. Drop caps are large characters that drop below the first baseline. In InDesign this is specified by a the number of lines you want the character to "drop"—the more lines specified, the larger the character.

This drop cap is customized by placing an outlined lowercase letter on top of the text frame (Type –> Create Outlines). A blending mode of Multiply has been applied using the Effects panel.

While setting automated drop caps can be a real time saver, it introduces legibility issues like ugly spacing around certain letter forms.

DROP CAPS ARE USED TO INDICATE OPENING section starts or paragraphs in a document, and are not used for consecutive paragraphs. Drop caps are large characters that drop below the first baseline. In InDesign this is specified by a the number of lines you want the character to "drop"—the more lines specified, the larger the character.

Notice how the text wraps to the contour of the drop cap.

DROP CAPS ARE USED TO INDICATE OPENING section starts or paragraphs in a document, and are not used for consecutive paragraphs. Drop caps are large characters that drop below the first baseline. In InDesign this is specified by a the number of lines you want the character to "drop"—the more lines specified, the larger the character.

The outlined character is placed in position.

A rough zero pt stroke width shape is drawn.

DROP CAPS ARE USED TO INDICATE OPENING section starts or paragraphs in a document, and are not used for consecutive paragraphs. Drop caps are large characters that drop below the first baseline. In InDesign this is specified by a the number of lines you want the character to "drop"—the more lines specified, the larger the character.

A text wrap is applied to the shape to push the text away from it and the drop cap.

DROP CAPS ARE USED TO INDICATE OPENING section starts or paragraphs in a document, and are not used for consecutive paragraphs. Drop caps are large characters that drop below the first baseline. In InDesign this is specified by a the number of lines you want the character to "drop"—the more lines specified, the larger the character.

A customized drop cap created from characters and ornaments—outlined and then unified using pathfinders—with *fx* applied (bevel and emboss, drop shadow).

Drop cap is used to indicate an opening section start or paragraph in a document and is not used for consecutive paragraphs. Drop caps are large characters that drop below the first baseline. In InDesign this is specified by a the number of lines you want the character to "drop"—the more lines specified, the larger the character.

Bullets and Numbering

Bullets and numbers are used to organize information. While the default "•" bullet character is defined by the typeface used and automatically applied, you can also choose to insert custom bullets. Any character from any font can be used to do this. You can create multi-level bulleted lists using styles with indents.

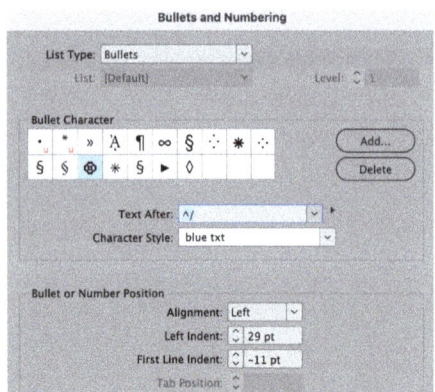

Any character from any font can be used as a bullet. All characters except for the first default one can be deleted from the menu.

- This is InDesign's default bullet style. It uses a tab for spacing (^t). You should change this to something more legible.
- This bullet style is based on the default, using a small indent and a *figure space* for spacing (^/).
  - This multi-level bullet point uses a larger indent. These first three bulleted paragraphs have Paragraph Shading gratuitously applied.

> ⊙ A bullet symbol (from Adobe Aldine) is used for the bullet and a character style colors it.
> ⊙ **A bullet symbol (from Adobe Aldine) is used for the bullet**: and a nested style for the bold text (defined by the colon ":").
> ▶ This bullet uses a right pointing triangle (from Minion Pro) and a character style to color it.
> ▶ **This bullet style with colored bold text uses a right pointing triangle (from Minion Pro) and a character style to color it.**
> o This bullet uses a bullet symbol (from Minion Pro) and a character style to color it.

For multi-level lists, create a paragraph style for each level of the list, and apply where appropriate. The paragraph styles used here are called *numbers list L1*, *L2* and *L3* corresponding to their levels. If you are importing a Word or RTF document that already has an application generated numbered list, InDesign will honor it and automatically create the list entries.

numbers list L1

numbers list L2

numbers list L3

Any Bulleted or Numbered list can be converted to text (Type > Bulleted & Numbered Lists > Convert Bullets and Numbering to Text).

1. The first item in this list (numbers list L1 style)
   A. An additional point for this entry (numbers list L2 style)
      a. Another point for the additional point (numbers list L3 style)
2. The second item in this list (numbers list L1 style)
   A. Another point for the second item (numbers list L2 style)

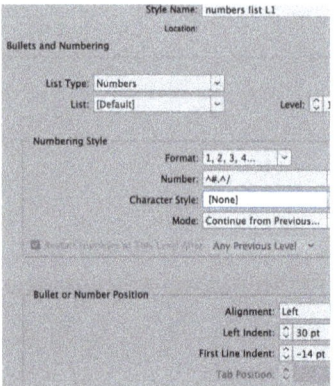 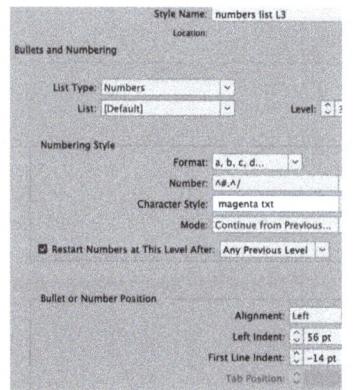 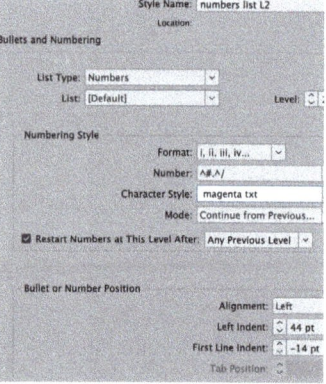

Tabs

Tabs are hard spaces measured from the left edge of a text frame. They are used to consistently create alignments within similar paragraphs. This "hard space" means that if your tab setting is wider than your column width it will wrap to the next line. Tabs can be justified to the left (text will follow it), center (text will be centered under it), right (text will precede it), or to a decimal or other specified character text will be aligned to it).

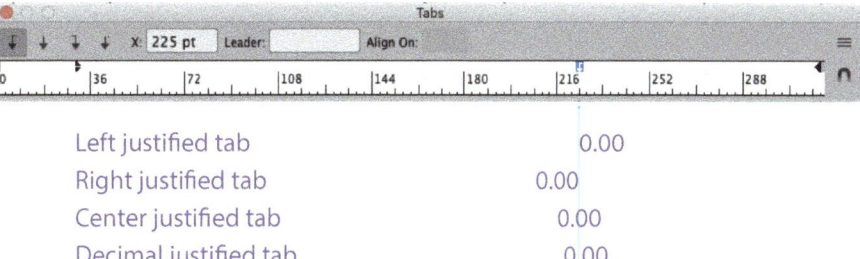

> All tabs are set to the same x position

Left justified tab	0.00
Right justified tab	0.00
Center justified tab	0.00
Decimal justified tab	0.00

Note that tabs have to be physically added to the text in order for them to be applied— the text won't magically move; you have to press the tab key. Tab leaders, usually dots but they could be any character pasted into the Leader box, may be used to visually guide the eye to the tabbed content.

> You can do this, but should you…? A character style is applied to the tab to highlight it's leader characters.

Left justified tab	0.00
Right justified tab > > > > > > > >	0.00
Center justified tab |||||||||||||||||||||||||	0.00
Decimal justified tab ~~~~~~~~~~~~~~~~	0.00

Tab leaders are often used in menu layouts to indicate prices:

> ***Diavolo Chicken*** — Succulent pieces of fire-grilled chicken marinated in black pepper, cilantro, garlic and lime. Served over a bed of fragrant rice, and topped with a sublime Mint Juju Sauce. $15.95

Tabs can be used for tabular data with more than one item in a line. The reverse type header uses a first line indent and tabs visually aligned with decimal tabs below it:

Shipping	First Item	Add'l Items
U.S. - economy (1-2 weeks)	$3.50	+$1.00
U.S. - express (2 days)	$6.00	+$2.00
U.S. - express (overnight)	$15.00	+$3.00

Other uses for tabs are found in tables of contents (TOC). Tabbed text can also be converted to tables.

Keep Options

Keep Options may be applied to heading styles to keep the headings with the paragraph that follows them. If not part of a style, they can be applied locally from the drop-down menu in the Paragraph panel. Text paragraphs can also use Keep Options to prevent orphans and widows:

At least two lines of a paragraph should remain with its heading in order to avoid any possible crimes against typography—one line is also acceptable if there are space constraints. Use Keep Options to specify the number of lines that need to remain with the heading. Keep Options can force a jump to a new column, new frame or new page.

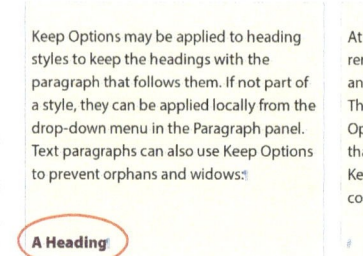

With no Keep Options applied, the heading is cruelly isolated from its following paragraph.

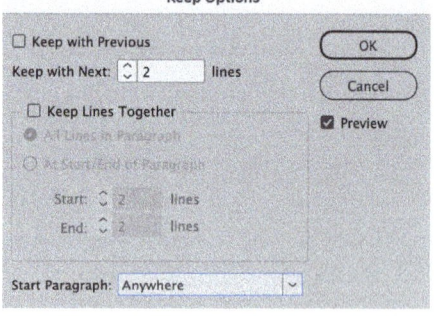

Setting the Keep Options forces the heading to stay with the paragraph. You can specify up to five lines or a whole paragraph to be "kept".

Table of Contents (TOC)

Do not make a manual TOC, let InDesign do it for you. InDesign generates TOCs based on paragraph styles. You should define these as early as you can and make them part of your proofing process to avoid mistakes down the line, especially for long documents. Obviously, if your styles are not applied correctly for the TOC, they will be inaccurate.

TOCs can also be used to generate indexes. This is sometimes easier than manually inserting index markers into the text, since it pulls from styles that are already applied to your document. This is particularly true when working with catalogs where a product name may already be formatted by a paragraph style. You can generate an index of products by creating a TOC that targets the product name style.

TOC *styles* are helpful if you want to have multiple TOCs used in the same document. For example, a catalog may need a TOC for section headers, a different one for the product index, and your client may want to generate a list of SKUs and the pages they are on to verify that all the products are being used as intended. You'll have three TOC styles. Similarly, it's common in nonfiction books and proposals to need a list of figures and tables. These are easy to make when you have paragraph styles for them.

Character Styles

¶ Let character styles do as little as possible. If not used in conjunction with paragraph styles, characters need to be selected in order to have styles applied to them. Character Style attributes will override similar ones in Paragraph styles. For example, if your paragraph style uses 12 pt type, applying a character style with a different size will make the selection that size. A character style's leading will also override a paragraphs leading for the line or lines it appears in. This will affect the line spacing if the leading is greater than the paragraph style's, forcing a jump to the next available baseline to which it can snap.

This paragraph uses 11 pt type with 14 pt leading.

The bold character style uses 12 pt type but has no leading associated with it.

These gaps are caused by a Character Style's leading being greater than that of the paragraph style. Align to Grid is on.

The small caps character style uses 10 pt type with 15 pt leading, forcing it to jump to the next available baseline, effectively at 28 pts.

Character Style attributes will override similar ones in Paragraph styles. For example, if your paragraph style uses 12 pt type, applying a character style with a **different size** will make the selection that size. A character style's leading, if it has been assigned, will also OVERRIDE A PARAGRAPH'S LEADING for the line or lines it appears in.

If the text is not snapped to the baseline, alignment will still become irregular where a different leading has been used:

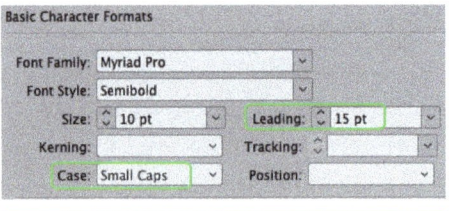

The grid don't lie…
The big bold text is 12/14
The small caps are 11/15, causing misalignment.

Character Style attributes will override similar ones in Paragraph styles. For example, if your paragraph style uses 12 pt type, applying a character style with a **different size** will make the selection that size. A character style's leading, if it has been assigned, will also OVERRIDE A PARAGRAPH'S LEADING for the line or lines it appears in.

Sometimes it is useful to not specify a font family when creating a character style. Font styles like Regular, Italic, Bold are common to most serif and sans serif typefaces. Creating styles that use just these attributes can be applied to any typeface, and if the attribute exists in the font, it will be applied

The same "bold" and "italic" styles are applied to these typefaces. Since Felt Tip Roman does not have these instances, they have been ignored.

Myriad Pro: Bold text precedes the regular text, and *italicized text comes after it.*

Felt Tip Roman: Bold text precedes the regular text, and italicized text comes after it.

Times New Roman: Bold text precedes the regular text, and *italicized text comes after it.*

If the font does not support it, it won't be applied. Be careful when setting character styles since something available in one font may not be available in another.

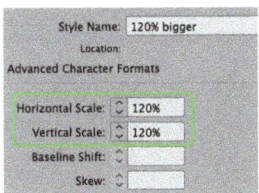

Character styles can also be used to scale text within a paragraph or highlight it. Scaling is applied in the *Advanced Character Formats* sub panel using vertical and horizontal scaling (this example also has a color applied to it).

The highlight is created by applying an underline the same weight or larger than the type size (*Basic Character Formats* sub panel) and offsetting it to visually balance it with the text:

Since no typeface attributes have been set, the scaling or highlight can be applied to any text without altering the base font. Note that since underlines are a fixed width, as the size of the type gets bigger the highlight will appear to be skinnier and cover less of the text.

This 14 pt text has an 8 pt underline applied.

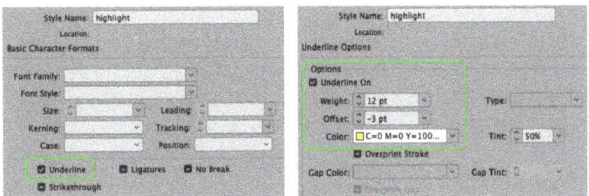

Note: using underlines as a paragraph style will apply the underline to the whole paragraph.

Small Caps

Since small caps are often scaled-down versions of a typeface, they can sometimes look a little thin when compared to body text. The default setting for small caps scaling is set in the *Advanced Type* sub panel in *Preferences*. Typically, small caps are created at the x-height of the typeface, but InDesign scales them from the point size. Since different typefaces at the same point size can appear to be bigger or smaller due to their x-heights, consider a scaling that visually fits with your font. The small cap scaling for this text, using Myriad Pro, is 75%.

Myriad Pro x-height   Baskerville x-height

MYRIAD PRO small caps

BASKERVILLE small caps

Notice how the Small Caps scaling (75% as set in Preferences) based on the type size affects the size of the small caps in typefaces with the same size (18 pt) but different x-heights.

Some OpenType typefaces have a specific SMALL CAPS version which you should write into your styles in order to use them—you'll know if it exists since it is a separate font and will be called something like Garamond Pro Small Caps. You could also substitute a **semibold** version if your typeface supports it, for some subtle emphasis.

regular SMALL CAPS regular text | semibold SMALL CAPS regular text

Using All Caps is considered extreme, LIKE SHOUTING IN A LIBRARY…

Object Styles

¶ ANY STROKE AND FILL ATTRIBUTES CAN BE saved as Object Styles, including effects like transparency, feathering or drop shadows. It is also possible to have separate stylings for stroke and fill: a frame's stroke may retain its opacity while its fill might be transparent. Paragraph styles can also be implemented via object styles for text frames.

> This frame has a solid stroke and a transparent fill. The text is automatically formatted by a paragraph style included in the object style

> This frame has a solid stroke and a transparent fill. The text has a gradient feather applied to make it fade into the background

> The whole frame, including the text has a gradient feather applied to it, making it fade

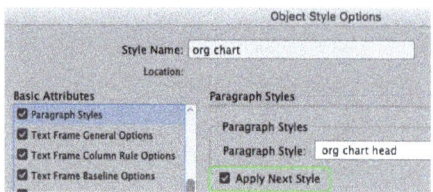

Using *Apply Next Style* in an object style's Paragraph Styles (Basic Attributes) settings allows for consistency in formatting, useful for things like name tags or organizational charts that have lots of different text frames that need to be the same size and have the same formatting:

Applying an object style to text frames unifies their design. The styled frames have been given a fixed size in the style. The paragraph style [1] for the shaded header (org chart head) has the *Next Style* attribute activated to apply the org chart name style [2], which also has an active *Next Style* to apply the org info style [3] in the last line.

Inspector
Dana Dingbat
Department of Ty-
pography Police

Detective
Halley Hyphen
Department of Typogra-
phy Police

Inspector	[1]	Detective
Dana Dingbat	[2]	Halley Hyphen
Department of Typography Police	[3]	Department of Typography Police

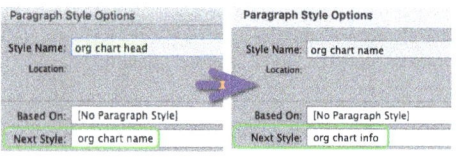

Next style is a feature that works in object-styled boxes: when paragraph styles have the next style applied, applying an object style to an unstyled frame will automatically apply those 'next' paragraph styles to the text.

Auto-Sizing text frames is very useful as an object style when the amount of text in a frame is variable. For example the sidebar text frames in this document use Height Only auto-sizing that push down as the amount of text in the frame increases. (The type style is also set in the object style).

Text frames may also benefit from auto-sizing that pushes the frame up when the bottom of a frame needs to be aligned to something…

This frame is one line deep

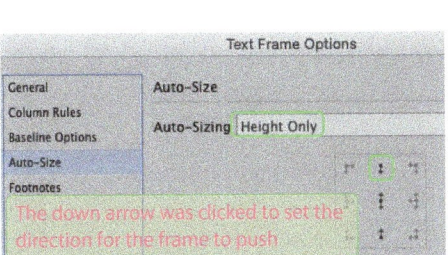

The down arrow was clicked to set the direction for the frame to push

But this frame grows as more text is added to it. Since the text is snapping to the baseline grid, the frame needs to be manually adjusted for balance by selecting it and using the arrow keys to move it up or down—the text won't move because it is snapped to the grid.

But this frame grows as more text is added to it. Since the text is snapping to the baseline grid, the frame needs to be manually adjusted for balance by selecting it and using the arrow keys to move it up or down—the text won't move because it is snapped to the grid.

… or when the width of the frame needs to be adaptive to the text:

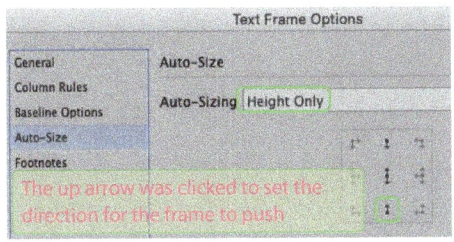

The up arrow was clicked to set the direction for the frame to push

A text frame can be made to push up as it fills with text,

A text frame can be made to push up as it fills with text, like this frame does—very useful if you want the **bottom** of the fame aligned to something.

You don't have to make styles to apply one-off attributes, but if you want to reuse them consistently, saving them as styles is easy and a great time-saver.

Styles saved to CC Libraries are accessible from any document.

This centered frame…

…expands equally on both sides to accommodate the text

This frame with right-aligned text…

… expands leftwards to accommodate the added text

Object Styles

Photos and thumbtacks include effects:
 → both have drop shadows
 → thumbtacks also have a bevel and emboss

Post-it note has a drop shadow

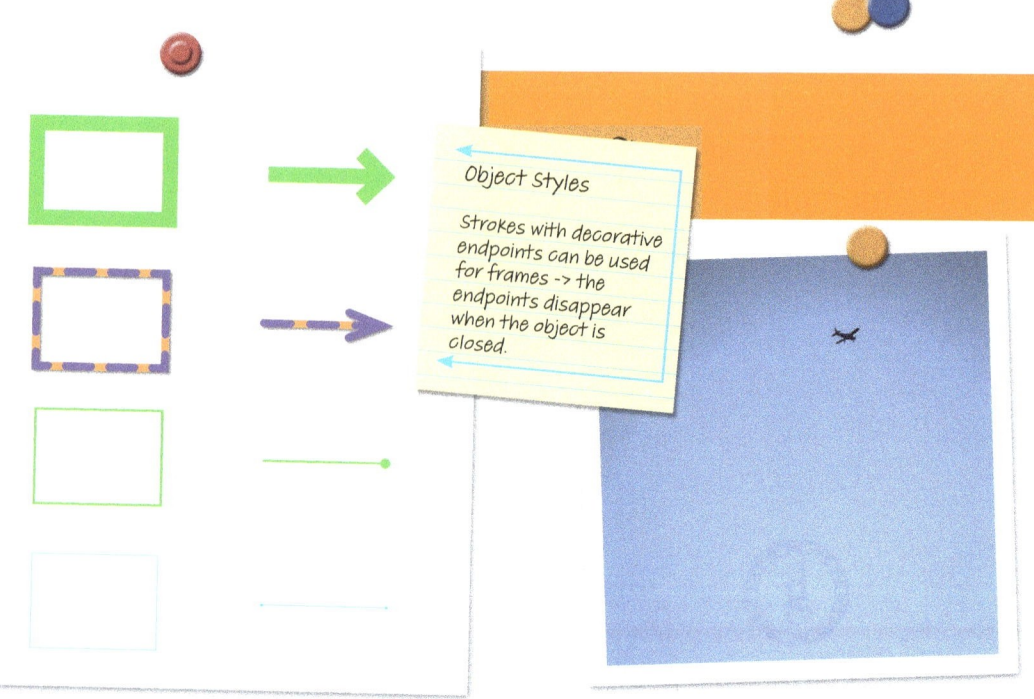

Object Styles

Strokes with decorative endpoints can be used for frames → the endpoints disappear when the object is closed.

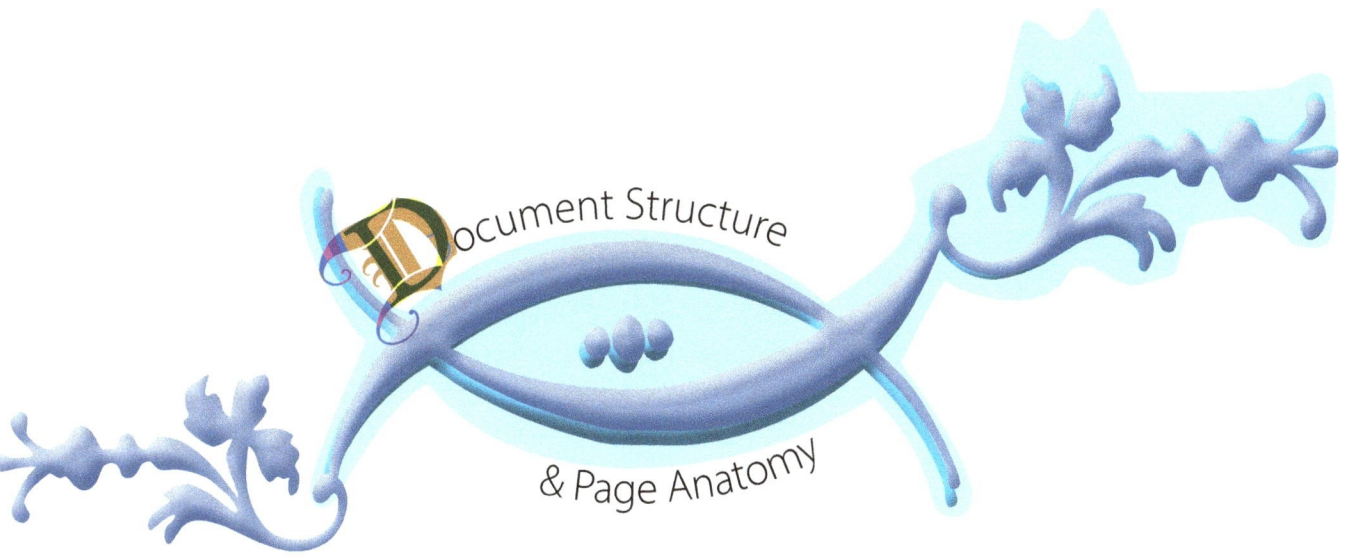

Document Structure & Page Anatomy

¶ Whether it is one page or 1000, it is essential to understand how to construct a document. Long documents often require a modified approach to make working with them or editing them easier. What is a long document? Anything that can be broken into sections or chapters, or content from multiple authors can be thought of as a "long" document. Think of magazines or books—multiple small sections that make a much larger whole. These sections or chapters should be created as separate independent files, like they are for this book. Any number of these files can be unified into what InDesign considers a book, with consistent styles and layout across all the pages. Document structure, the positioning of text and images on a page, the layout, is facilitated by the Parent pages. Applying a different Parent page reflows the text on that page to conform to the new Parent's structure, adopting whatever recurring Parent page elements it has, like page numbers or the positioning and number of columns, to repeatable graphic styles and even text styles assigned to text frames.

Page Anatomy

Anatomy of a Page

The unformatted text below is used to show how typographic consistency is achieved by: The application of styles The use of grids Note: the pilchrow symbol "¶" is pasted into the unformatted text to indicate every time the return key has been pressed, creating forced line breaks. It is what you would see if you Show Hidden Characters (Type menu). To get text into InDesign you can Place it (File menu) if it is in a format like .txt, .doc, .rtf, or copy and paste it from some other source like a pdf. You can also place an InDesign file into another InDesign file. Check the Show Import Options box in the Place panel to select specific pages to place.

Typography Is Made Consistent With Styles ¶
This Is The "Sub Shaded" Paragraph Style ¶ This is the body no in style. It sits flush against the left margin, and follows a subheading. Quiaecea porepercid excea nonsequia quam, sita volum que volupta dolo es sa vel modipit sita volum que volupta atibeat. ¶
This is the body in style. It has a first line indent to push the text away from the left margin and create a visual cue that a new paragraph has been created. Ommodit et veri raectaquae qui tota accae cum nissenduntur millut quaepercil min plaut autem explabo. ¶
Another Subheading Style ¶
This is the body no in space after style. The "space after" automatically creates one line of space between the paragraphs. Ipsapis rerovid quat volorum repuda volore, sere officius ped quiduci istesequi to to tetur, sin nulparit, quiaspedit quate conseque officium nonsecatem. ¶
This is the body no in space after style. The "space after" automatically creates one line of space between the paragraphs. Ipsapis rerovid quat volorum repuda volore, sere officius ped quiduci istesequi to to tetur, sin nulparit, quiaspedit quate conseque officium nonsecatem. ¶
Spaced Out Bullets ¶
This is the indented bullets SA style with space after the paragraph ¶
pro conectur ¶
id ma doloris sit ¶
Tight Bullets ¶
Enihit imoluptas endis mo es esciis quos ese vellit aut rem ipsapis rerovid quat volorum repuda volore, sere officius ped quiduci istesequi to to tetur, sin nulparit, quiaspedit quate conseque officium nonsecatem: ¶
This is the indented bullets style no space after the paragraph ¶
 pro conectur ¶
id ma doloris sit ¶

The examples on the following pages show:
- Parent Page set up
- Formatted text as it appears on a page
- Formatted text on the Baseline and Document grids
- A breakdown of the styles used

Anatomy of a Parent Page

This is the underlying document structure. Margins and columns are set up on the Parent Page when the document is created. Additional Parent pages are set up after the document has been created.

These guides are subsequently set up on the Parent Page.

More complex guides can also be created (Layout > Create Guides…) on Parent pages or individual pages as needed, although not needed on these pages.

These footer elements are also on the Parent Page so that they repeat on every page based on that Parent. To use different Parent Pages that have the same Parent elements, simply copy them and then Paste in Place (Edit menu) onto the new Parent Page.

Typography Is Made Consistent With Styles

This Is The "Sub Shaded" Paragraph Style

This is the *body no in style*. It sits flush against the left margin, and follows a subheading. Quiaecea porepercid excea nonsequia quam, sita volum que volupta dolo es sa vel modipit sita volum que volupta atibeat.

This is the *body in style.* It has a first line indent to push the text away from the left margin and create a visual cue that a new paragraph has been created. Ommodit et veri raectaquae qui tota accae cum nissenduntur millut quaepercil min plaut autem explabo.

Another Subheading Style

This is the *body no in space after style*. The "space after" automatically creates one line of space between the paragraphs. Ipsapis rerovid quat volorum repuda volore, sere officius ped quiduci istesequi to to tetur, sin nulparit, quiaspedit quate conseque officium nonsecatem.

This is the *body no in space after style*. The "space after" automatically creates one line of space between the paragraphs. Ipsapis rerovid quat volorum repuda volore, sere officius ped quiduci istesequi to to tetur, sin nulparit, quiaspedit quate conseque officium nonsecatem.

Spaced Out Bullets

- This is the *indented bullets SA style* with space after the paragraph

- pro conectur id ma doloris sit

Tight Bullets

Enihit imoluptas endis mo es esciis quos ese vellit aut rem ipsapis rerovid quat volorum repuda volore, sere officius ped quiduci istesequi to to tetur, sin nulparit, quiaspedit quate conseque officium nonsecatem:

- This is the *indented bullets style* no space after the paragraph
- pro conectur id ma doloris sit

Viewing the Baseline Grid

This Is The "Sub Shaded" Paragraph Style

This is the *body no in style*. It sits flush against the left margin, and follows a **subheading.** Quiaecea porepercid excea nonsequia quam, sita volum que volupta dolo es sa vel modipit sita volum que volupta atibeat.

   This is the *body in style*. **It has a first line indent to push the text away from the left margin and create a visual cue that a new paragraph has been created.** Ommodit et veri raectaquae qui tota accae cum nissenduntur millut quaepercil min plaut autem explabo.

Another Subheading Style

This is the *body no in space after style*. **The "space after" automatically creates one line of space between the paragraphs.** Ipsapis rerovid quat volorum repuda volore, sere officius ped quiduci istesequi to to tetur, sin nulparit, quiaspedit quate conseque officium nonsecatem.

This is the *body no in space after style*. **The "space after" automatically creates one line of space between the paragraphs.** Ipsapis rerovid quat volorum repuda volore, sere officius ped quiduci istesequi to to tetur, sin nulparit, quiaspedit quate conseque officium nonsecatem.

Spaced Out Bullets

- This is the *indented bullets SA style* with space after the paragraph

- pro conectur id ma doloris sit

Tight Bullets

Enihit imoluptas endis mo es esciis quos ese vellit aut rem ipsapis rerovid quat volorum repuda volore, sere officius ped quiduci istesequi to to tetur, sin nulparit, quiaspedit quate conseque officium nonsecatem:

- This is the *indented bullets style* no space after the paragraph
- pro conectur id ma doloris sit

Document type is 10 pt
Document leading is 14 pt
Margins are 54 pt (0.75 in) for Top, Right, and Bottom; 180 pt (2.5 in) for Left.
All type snaps to the Baseline Grid.

The grid is created in *Preferences (cmd/ctrl + K) > Grids…*
Start at 0
Increment 14 pt (same as leading)
The Grids in Back check box is unchecked to keep all the grid lines above text and image frames To show/hide the baseline grid:
cmd +option + '
ctrl + alt + '

Viewing the Document Grid

This Is The "Sub Shaded" Paragraph Style

This is the *body no in style*. It sits flush against the left margin, and follows a subheading. Quiaecea porepercid excea nonsequia quam, sita volum que volupta dolo es sa vel modipit sita volum que volupta atibeat.

This is the *body in style.* It has a first line indent to push the text away from the left margin and create a visual cue that a new paragraph has been created. Ommodit et veri raectaquae qui tota accae cum nissenduntur millut quaepercil min plaut autem explabo.

Another Subheading Style

This is the *body no in space after style*. The "space after" automatically creates one line of space between the paragraphs. Ipsapis rerovid quat volorum repuda volore, sere officius ped quiduci istesequi to to tetur, sin nulparit, quiaspedit quate conseque officium nonsecatem.

This is the *body no in space after style*. The "space after" automatically creates one line of space between the paragraphs. Ipsapis rerovid quat volorum repuda volore, sere officius ped quiduci istesequi to to tetur, sin nulparit, quiaspedit quate conseque officium nonsecatem.

Spaced Out Bullets

- This is the *indented bullets SA style* with space after the paragraph

- pro conectur id ma doloris sit

Tight Bullets

Enihit imoluptas endis mo es esciis quos ese vellit aut rem ipsapis rerovid quat volorum repuda volore, sere officius ped quiduci istesequi to to tetur, sin nulparit, quiaspedit quate conseque officium nonsecatem:

- This is the *indented bullets style* no space after the paragraph
- pro conectur id ma doloris sit

The Document Grid (graph paper) is set to align with the baseline grid: If you don't want square graph paper, change the number of vertical subdivisions to create rectangles. You can Show/Hide the Document Grid: cmd/ctrl + '

Gridline every 140 pts
10 subdivisions
The Grids in Back check box is unchecked to keep all the grid lines above text and image frames.

Typography Is Made Consistent With Styles

This Is The "Sub Shaded" Paragraph Style

This is the *body no in style*. It sits flush against the left margin, and follows a subheading. Quiaecea poperpercid excea nonsequia quam, sita volum que volupta dolo es sa vel modipit sita volum que volupta atibeat.
 This is the *body in style.* It has a first line indent to push the text away from the left margin and create a visual cue that a new paragraph has been created. Ommodit et veri raectaquae qui tota accae cum nissenduntur millut quaepercil min plaut autem explabo.

Another Subheading Style

This is the *body no in space after style*. The "space after" automatically creates one line of space between the paragraphs. Ipsapis rerovid quat volorum repuda volore, sere officius ped quiduci istesequi to to tetur, sin nulparit, quiaspedit quate conseque officium nonsecatem.

This is the *body no in space after style*. The "space after" automatically creates one line of space between the paragraphs. Ipsapis rerovid quat volorum repuda volore, sere officius ped quiduci istesequi to to tetur, sin nulparit, quiaspedit quate conseque officium nonsecatem.

Spaced Out Bullets

- This is the *indented bullets SA style* with space after the paragraph

- pro conectur id ma doloris sit

Tight Bullets

Enihit imoluptas endis mo es esciis quos ese vellit aut rem ipsapis rerovid quat volorum repuda volore, sere officius ped quiduci istesequi to to tetur, sin nulparit, quiaspedit quate conseque officium nonsecatem:

- This is the *indented bullets style* no space after the paragraph
- pro conectur id ma doloris sit

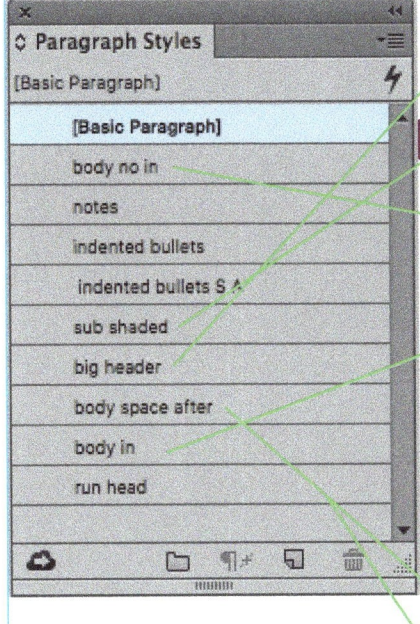

These styles are applied in this document

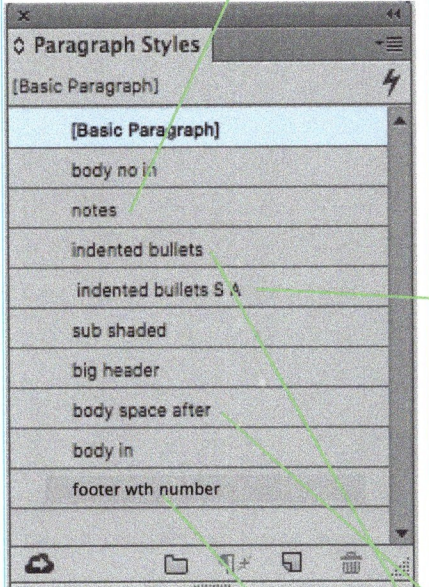

The locally formatted text (magenta italics, gray text) are *Character Styles*. The bulleted paragraph styles have a character style nested within them to apply the color to the bullet

Show Hidden Characters is simulated by the ¶ pasted in at the end of each paragraph

Objects on the Parent page are indicated by a thin dotted-line frame

Guide to Typography + InDesign

Typography Is Made Consistent With Styles

This Is The "Sub Shaded" Paragraph Style

This is the *body no in style*. It sits flush against the left margin, and follows a subheading. Quiaecea porepercid excea nonsequia quam, sita volum que volupta dolo es sa vel modipit sita volum que volupta atibeat.

   This is the *body in style*. It has a first line indent to push the text away from the left margin and create a visual cue that a new paragraph has been created. Ommodit et veri raectaquae qui tota accae cum nissenduntur millut quaepercil min plaut autem explabo.

Another Subheading Style

This is the *body no in space after style*. The "space after" automatically creates one line of space between the paragraphs. Ipsapis rerovid quat volorum repuda volore, sere officius ped quiduci istesequi to to tetur, sin nulparit, quiaspedit quate conseque officium nonsecatem.

This is the *body no in space after style*. The "space after" automatically creates one line of space between the paragraphs. Ipsapis rerovid quat volorum repuda volore, sere officius ped quiduci istesequi to to tetur, sin nulparit, quiaspedit quate conseque officium nonsecatem.

Spaced Out Bullets

- This is the *indented bullets SA style* with space after the paragraph

- pro conectur id ma doloris sit

Tight Bullets

Enihit imoluptas endis mo es esciis quos ese vellit aut rem ipsapis rerovid quat volorum repuda volore, sere officius ped quiduci istesequi to to tetur, sin nulparit, quiaspedit quate conseque officium nonsecatem:

- This is the *indented bullets style* no space after the paragraph
- pro conectur id ma doloris sit

Annotations (margin notes):

- These Paragraph Styles do not have *Space After* applied to them. A *First Line Indent* is used to indicate a new paragraph.
- These paragraphs have a *Space After* applied in the Paragraph Style. It equals the leading.
- The custom bullet ⊙ is added in the paragraph style, from the Add pull-down menu. The color is applied as a Character Style. These bullets have a *Space After* applied to them.
- These bullets don't have a *Space After* applied to them
- Guide [so that important items don't get swallowed in the binding: it matches the right margin width] Text frame margin
- Page numbers (Marker) created on Parent page

Guide to Typography + InDesign | 40

Auto Style and Style Packs

Style Packs can be a time saver for auto-formatting documents with relatively few paragraph styles. Even if your styles are not all supported, you can later physically apply the additional paragraph styles where needed. Style Packs support the following styles:

- One heading
- One subheading
- One paragraph
- One bullet
- Two numbered lists l

f your document falls within these formatting parameters, Auto Styling may be a great time saver (Type > Auto Style). You can build your own style pack or modify an existing one (Window > Styles > Style Packs), however, *Next Style* within a paragraph style is not supported. And while you can "trick" a numbered list into being a bulleted one, this is not a practical workaround.

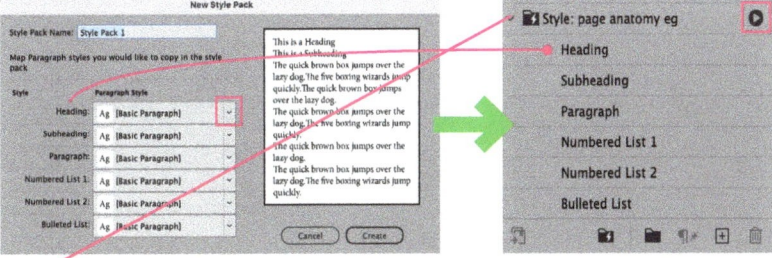

You can map any of your existing styles, using the dropdown menu next to each style, to the ones in the Style Pack. The styles names, however, remain the same as the ones in the pack.

This is a Heading

This is a Subheading

This is a Paragraph where the quick brown fox jumps over the lazy dog. The Five boxing wizards jump quickly. The quick brown fox jumps over the lazy dog.

§ The quick brown fox jumps over the lazy dog.
1. The Five boxing wizards jump quickly.
   i. The quick brown fox jumps over the lazy dog.

This is a Heading
This is a Subheading
This is a Paragraph where the quick brown fox jumps over the lazy dog. The Five boxing wizards jump quickly. The quick brown fox jumps over the lazy dog.
• The quick brown fox jumps over the lazy dog.
1. The Five boxing wizards jump quickly.
1.1 The quick brown fox jumps over the lazy dog.

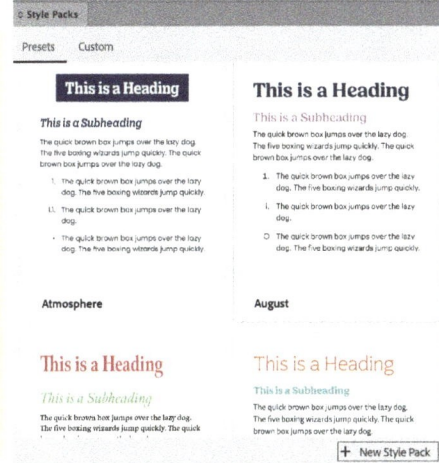

To apply a Style Pack place the Type Tool cursor within the text and click the style you want in the Style Pack panel, or on the "play" arrow next to the style pack name on the Paragraph Styles panel. There are issues with the auto styling not activating fonts and not applying the style. It may be more effective to build your own pack based on fonts in your system or that you want to use and are activated. You may still need to manually apply the styles that auto styling has missed.

Typography With Style Packs

This Is The "Subheading" Paragraph Style

> Style Packs *do not* honor Next Style, so the First Line Indent has not been applied to the following paragraph.

This is the Paragraph style (based on *body no in*). It sits flush against the left margin, and follows a subheading. Quiaecea porepercid excea nonsequia quam, sita volum que volupta dolo es sa vel modipit sita volum que volupta atibeat.
This should be the body in style. It has *not* been applied since Style Packs do not honor Next Styles, and only support one paragraph style, so the first line indent, the visual cue for a new paragraph, has not been created.

Another Subheading

This should be the body space after style. The "space after" would automatically create one line of space between the paragraphs, but it has not since *only one paragraph style is supported* in Style Packs.

> *Style Packs only support one paragraph style*. Additional styles need to be applied manually.

This should also be the body space after style. The "space after" would automatically create one line of space between the paragraphs, but it has not since only one paragraph style is supported in Style Packs. Ipsapis rerovid quat volorum repuda volore, sere officius ped quiduci istesequi to to tetur, sin nulparit, quiaspedit quate conseque officium nonsecatem.

Bullets

- This is the Bulleted List style with no space between the bulleted paragraphs. The last bullet is followed by an empty Paragaraph to push the heading that follows down one line
- Enihit imoluptas endis mo es esciis quos ese vellit aut rem ipsapis rerovid quat volorum repuda volore, sere officius ped quiduci istesequi to to tetur, sin nulparit, quiaspedit quate conseque officium nonsecatem
- pro conectur
- id ma doloris sit

Numbered List

1. This is the Numbered List 1 style, in the Style Pack. Style Pack names cannot be changed, doing so disables Auto Style,
   i. This is the Numbered List 2 style, in the Style Pack. Style Pack numbered lists only support two levels.

2. Pro conectur
   i. Id ma doloris sit

Style Packs And Regular Styles

This Is The "Subheading" Paragraph Style

This is the Paragrpah style (based on body no in). It sits flush against the left margin, and follows a subheading. Quiaecea porepercid excea nonsequia quam, sita volum que volupta dolo es sa vel modipit sita volum que volupta atibeat.

This is the body in style, applied manually, since Style Packs do not honor Next Styles, and only support one paragraph style, so the first line indent, the visual cue for a new paragraph, has not been created.

> The "body in" style is manually applied after Auto Styling.

Another Subheading

This is the manually applied body space after style which automatically creates a line of space between paragraphs. It has to be manually applied since only one paragraph style is supported in Style Packs.

This is also be the body space after style. The "space after" automatically creates one line of space between the paragraphs. Ipsapis rerovid quat volorum repuda volore, sere officius ped quiduci istesequi to to tetur, sin nulparit, quiaspedit quate conseque officium nonsecatem.

> Style Packs only support one paragraph style. So to get this layout to look like the other examples, additional styles would need to be applied manually.

Bullets

- This is the Bulleted List style with no space between the bulleted paragraphs. The last bullet is followed by an empty Paragaraph to push the heading that follows down one line
- Enihit imoluptas endis mo es esciis quos ese vellit aut rem ipsapis rerovid quat volorum repuda volore, sere officius ped quiduci istesequi to to tetur, sin nulparit, quiaspedit quate conseque officium nonsecatem
- Pro conectur
- Id ma doloris sit

Numbered List

1. This is the Numbered List 1 style in the Style Pack. Style Pack names cannot be changed, doing so disables Auto Style,
    i. This is the Numbered List 2 style in the Style Pack. Style Pack numbered lists only support two levels.

2. Pro conectur
    i. Id ma doloris sit
        a. This third-level numbered list has been applied manually.

> Auto Styled lists only support two indented levels. Any additional levels need to be applied manually.

TABLES

¶ THERE ARE TIMES WHEN YOU WILL NEED to format comparative data, like product feature comparisons, data that changes over time, or to break information up into easily digestible chunks. Tables are a useful way to deal with such repetitive data. Oftentimes, this information will be given to you as a MS Excel or MS Word document. Word docs may also sometimes have excessive formatting added for alignment appearances— things like multiple tabs when one will do or multiple spaces instead of tabs. InDesign can import formatted text from Microsoft documents, substituting tab stops for columns and hard returns for rows. Sometimes it may be necessary to strip out all imported text formatting and reapply it using InDesign styles: InDesign supports formatted table styles which can include paragraph and character styles.

Below is an example using data that is separated by tabs and forced line breaks/returns: the table's columns will be defined by tabs and its rows by paragraphs. In each paragraph (row) there is only *one* tab separating the data for the columns.

Text is converted into a table under the Table menu: Table –> Convert Text to Table. It does not have to be in its own text frame.

The unformatted tabbed text…

```
                    2018    2019    2020    2021    2022    2023
GDP (at constant prices)    -4.4    -10.9    8.8    9.0    9.2    8.9
Domestic demand (contribution to growth)    -6.5    -16.9    10.4    11.1    9.4    9.0
Net exports (contribution to growth)    2.1    6.0    -1.5    -2.1    -0.2    -0.3
Per capita GDP (SUS, thousands)    7.4    2.5    3.5    4.0    4.6    4.2
Consumer prices (average)    -1.1    25.9    13.4    4.4    9.6    9.4
Consumer prices (end-of-period)    -1.5    41.0    3.7    4.4    9.6    9.0
```

… is formatted using styles.

Decimal tabs have been used align the numbers correctly. In an InDesign Table numerical text would be aligned to the right of the cell. This text will next be converted to a table.

Note that for smaller data blocks paragraph formatting may be all that is required, rather than actual Table formatting.

	2018	2019	2020	2021	2022	2023
GDP (at constant prices)	-4.4	-10.9	8.8	9.0	9.2	8.9
Domestic demand (contribution to growth)	-6.5	-16.9	10.4	11.1	9.4	9.0
Net exports (contribution to growth)	2.1	6.0	-1.5	-2.1	-0.2	-0.3
Per capita GDP (SUS, thousands)	7.4	2.5	3.5	4.0	4.6	4.2
Consumer prices (average)	-1.1	25.9	13.4	4.4	9.6	9.4
Consumer prices (end-of-period)	-1.5	41.0	3.7	4.4	9.6	9.0

Stroke Options

Strokes can be either conduits that guide the eye through information, or they can be clear borders to define where certain types of information begin and end. Remove barriers like pronounced vertical rules in what should be left-to- right data in the flow of information, unless they serve a specific organizational purpose.

The text is converted to a table organized by strokes. The formatted table can be saved as a Table Style.

Table –> Table Options –> Alternating Row Strokes/Alternating Column Strokes

Saved table and cell styles can be applied it to other data to achieve a consistency of design.

There is one important difference between text styles and table styles. Unlike character style attributes which can be part of a paragraph style, cell style attributes *are not part* of the table style. For example, you cannot use a table style to change the border color of interior cells. Instead, a cell style is created and included within the table style.

	2015	2016	2017	2018	2019	2020
GDP (at constant prices)	-4.4	-10.9	8.8	9.0	9.2	8.9
Domestic demand (contribution to growth)	-6.5	-16.9	10.4	11.1	9.4	9.0
Net exports (contribution to growth)	2.1	6.0	-1.5	-2.1	-0.2	-0.3
Per capita GDP (SUS, thousands)	7.4	2.5	3.5	4.0	4.6	4.2
Consumer prices (average)	-1.1	25.9	13.4	4.4	9.6	9.4
Consumer prices (end-of-period)	-1.5	41.0	3.7	4.4	9.6	9.0

For example, heavy row strokes create open channels that encourage left-to-right eye movement. This is an effective in presenting information that goes in that direction. Strong column strokes impose a top-to-bottom order on information and direct readers down a column to a total or an average at the bottom. Where you don't use background tints, strokes become essential to anchoring data and highlighting key information. Where color defines areas in a table, use strokes sparingly, if at all.

Color

Use colors and their tints to organize data and link information. It's best to use a limited palette on tables. Two colors (and tints of those colors) for fills and strokes, plus the color of your text, should see you through most tables quite well. In more complex tables, however, purposeful use of additional colors can help indicate different categories of information. Always consider context where color is concerned, and what may be implied by its usage.

Alternating Fills are one of InDesign's most useful table design features. Subtle use of alternating color can go a long way toward differentiating between rows and columns and directing the eye. Ensure that alternating fills are an aid to readability, not an obstacle. Be sure there's a high contrast between the text in a table and any alternating fills .

	2015	2016	2017	2018	2019	2020
GDP (at constant prices)	-4.4	-10.9	8.8	9.0	9.2	8.9
Domestic demand (contribution to growth)	-6.5	-16.9	10.4	11.1	9.4	9.0
Net exports (contribution to growth)	2.1	6.0	-1.5	-2.1	-0.2	-0.3
Per capita GDP (SUS, thousands)	7.4	2.5	3.5	4.0	4.6	4.2
Consumer prices (average)	-1.1	25.9	13.4	4.4	9.6	9.4
Consumer prices (end-of-period)	-1.5	41.0	3.7	4.4	9.6	9.0

Table rows can be defined by Alternating Fills. Strokes may be colored. The top row is converted to a Header, and has a Cell Style applied to create the darker bar. Its stroke and fill colors are the same.

	2015	2016	2017	2018	2019	2020
GDP (at constant prices)	-4.4	-10.9	8.8	9.0	9.2	8.9
Domestic demand (contribution to growth)	-6.5	-16.9	10.4	11.1	9.4	9.0
Net exports (contribution to growth)	2.1	6.0	-1.5	-2.1	-0.2	-0.3
Per capita GDP (SUS, thousands)	7.4	2.5	3.5	4.0	4.6	4.2
Consumer prices (average)	-1.1	25.9	13.4	4.4	9.6	9.4
Consumer prices (end-of-period)	-1.5	41.0	3.7	4.4	9.6	9.0

Alignment Within Cells

Alignment is critical to quickly understanding how pieces of information in a table relate, and each alignment choice carries with it an implied meaning. We most easily understand numbers (like financial figures) to be larger or smaller than one another when they're aligned to the right. In many fonts, figure widths vary and cause numeric misalignment. Where possible, use mono-spaced fonts for number-heavy tables, or take advantage of the Tabular numeral options in OpenType fonts for better alignment. It's quicker to scan a column of numbers that are decimal- or right-aligned than left-aligned. Consistency is always preferable when presenting numbers. If some of the numbers in your tables have decimals, all of them should and they should also be to the same number of decimal points (even if it's ".0" or ".00").

Text Styles in Tables

While tables shouldn't need a lot of styles, you'll be most efficient and consistent if you manage table text through InDesign's styles. Consider varying the size, weight, and font of table text. Information should appear differently only when it should be considered in a different way (for example, totals, averages, or references against which other information is compared). Table text may be presented slightly smaller than accompanying body text. The small blocks of text lend themselves well to condensed fonts, which might be less effective in body copy.

Column Spacing

If any consecutive columns contain the same type of information (e.g. financial figures), their column widths should be consistent. Inconsistent column widths make certain information seem different than what surrounds it. After adjusting columns on-the-fly, select columns of equal significance and choose Distribute Columns Evenly from the Table menu, which divides the total width by the number of selected columns and re-assigns the column width values equally. There's a similar feature for rows (Distribute Rows Evenly), but it is better to consider basing row-height decisions on the Exactly and At Least options.

"Exactly" or "At Least" Settings

Some table decisions are made for you (fixed), and some offer a bit of room to play with (flexible). If you're comparing 100 companies in a table that spans five pages, you have a fixed decision because basic division dictates that you must fit 20 companies per page. InDesign provides options appropriate for both fixed and flexible situations in the row height settings which can be assigned a height that is an exact amount (i.e. one-quarter inch, or 18 points) or a height of at least a certain amount.

All text inside cells can be formatted using any character or paragraph attributes. Use Paragraph Alignment buttons in the Control Bar or Paragraph Panel to align text within cells.

Numbers are best aligned to the right if they need to be understood relative to other numbers.

Right Aligned Numbers

9.0	9.2	8.9
11.1	9.4	9.0
-2.1	-0.2	-0.3

Left Aligned Numbers

9.0	9.2	8.9
11.1	9.4	9.0
-2.1	-0.2	-0.3

With fixed decisions, the Exactly setting will probably serve you best. Setting rows to an exact height allows not only consistency, but the ability to rely on simple math to make your content fit a given space. Bear in mind, however, that *exactly* means exactly. If your text doesn't fit in that row height, it will be overset. The cell will not adjust with the Exactly option applied.

For more flexible situations, the At Least setting can be very helpful, and it provides its own kind of consistency (but with flexibility). Setting a row height to At Least puts a mandatory minimum on that row. It can get bigger than the value you put in, but it can't get any smaller.

Anchored Objects and Graphic Cells

You can anchor objects into cells to guide the visual flow:

The blue triangle is positioned to overlap the white cell on the right. It is then anchored into the text in the blue cell on the left. This is repeated for each row of the table.

	2018	2019	2020	2021	2022	2023
GDP (at constant prices)	-4.4	-10.9	8.8	9.0	9.2	8.9
Domestic demand (contribution to growth)	-6.5	-16.9	10.4	11.1	9.4	9.0
Net exports (contribution to growth)	2.1	6.0	-1.5	-2.1	-0.2	-0.3
Per capita GDP (SUS, thousands)	7.4	2.5	3.5	4.0	4.6	4.2
Consumer prices (average)	-1.1	25.9	13.4	4.4	9.6	9.4
Consumer prices (end-of-period)	-1.5	41.0	3.7	4.4	9.6	9.0

The graphic icons are positioned to overlap the cell, grouped, and then anchored into one of the Header cells. They could also be individually anchored into each cell.

Code Adherence	Query Ratio	On-time Delivery	Use Capacity	Member Tier	Sector Segment
91.8%	0.50%	99.2%	93%	A	Private
90.1%	0.55%	97%	91%	B	Private
91.3%	0.052%	98.3%	94%	A	Public

In this example the grouped icons are pasted into a graphic cell. An empty row of cells are merged to create the single graphic cell (Table > Convert Cell to Graphic Cell).

Code Adherence	Query Ratio	On-time Delivery	Use Capacity	Member Tier	Sector Segment
91.8%	0.50%	99.2%	93%	A	Private
90.1%	0.55%	97%	91%	B	Private
91.3%	0.052%	98.3%	94%	A	Public

Cells can also have graphics placed into them if they are converted into graphic cells. (Table > Convert Cell to Graphic Cell). Individual cells can be merged into larger unified blocks.

New rows are inserted below the header and at the bottom of the table. Their cells are merged into one and then converted to graphic cells. (Table > Convert Cell to Graphic Cell). An image is placed into the graphic cells.

	2018	2019	2020	2021	2023	2023
GDP (at constant prices)	-4.4	-10.9	8.8	9.0	9.2	8.9
Domestic demand (contribution to growth)	-6.5	-16.9	10.4	11.1	9.4	9.0
Net exports (contribution to growth)	2.1	6.0	-1.5	-2.1	-0.2	-0.3
Per capita GDP (SUS, thousands)	7.4	2.5	3.5	4.0	4.6	4.2
Consumer prices (average)	-1.1	25.9	13.4	4.4	9.6	9.4
Consumer prices (end-of-period)	-1.5	41.0	3.7	4.4	9.6	9.0

Table Headers & Footers

InDesign automatically duplicates and inserts headers and footers for tables spanning multiple pages, frames or columns. (Table –> Table Options –> Headers and Footers). Headers identify the information that falls below them. They establish categorization and groupings.

These are designated Header and Footer rows. Headers are used to categorize the information of the columns below them.

	2018	2019	2020	2021	2022	2023
GDP (at constant prices)	-4.4	-10.9	8.8	9.0	9.2	8.9
Domestic demand (contribution to growth)	-6.5	-16.9	10.4	11.1	9.4	9.0
Net exports (contribution to growth)	2.1	6.0	-1.5	-2.1	-0.2	-0.3
Per capita GDP (SUS, thousands)	7.4	2.5	3.5	4.0	4.6	4.2
Consumer prices (average)	-1.1	25.9	13.4	4.4	9.6	9.4
Consumer prices (end-of-period)	-1.5	41.0	3.7	4.4	9.6	9.0
⋈						

Footers can serve many purposes (a simple source line, qualifying text for certain data elements in the table, etc.). Footers are not required for every table. Use if necessary.

Footers can contain any data, like the glyphs at the bottom of the table.

Notice how the Headers and Footers are repeated when the table is split to continue on the next page.

	2018	2019	2020	2021	2022	2023
GDP (at constant prices)	-4.4	-10.9	8.8	9.0	9.2	8.9
Domestic demand (contribution to growth)	-6.5	-16.9	10.4	11.1	9.4	9.0
Net exports (contribution to growth)	2.1	6.0	-1.5	-2.1	-0.2	-0.3
⋈						

Table continues on next page

Continuing from the previous page, the Header and Footer rows automatically repeat.

Table continues from previous page

	2018	2019	2020	2021	2022	2023
Per capita GDP (SUS, thousands)	7.4	2.5	3.5	4.0	4.6	4.2
Consumer prices (average)	-1.1	25.9	13.4	4.4	9.6	9.4
Consumer prices (end-of-period)	-1.5	41.0	3.7	4.4	9.6	9.0

Adjusting Tables

The Type tool is dynamic when working with tables. Use it to adjust table structure, move rows and columns, or change the table's style.

The Type tool cursor changes to indicate its function:

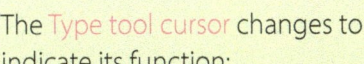 Selects a row, or a column

 Selects the whole table

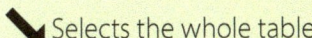 Moves a selected row or column

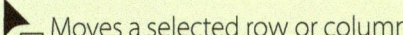 Moves a row or column border

▶ To move columns or rows, move the Text tool to the edge of the table until it turns into a black arrow. Click to select the column or row. Hover the cursor over the selection until it changes to the Table Pointer tool and then drag the selection into its new location. The cursor will also change to a double headed arrow when hovering over column or row borders to enable column or row adjustments. Note that this results in the overall table dimensions changing.

▶ Shift-drag to change a row or column without changing the table's size; option/alt-drag to add a row or column.

▶ Select the whole table in order to change its style: hover the cursor in the top left corner of the table until the Table Pointer tool is angled diagonally, then click to select it. Any saved styles in the Table Styles Panel can then be applied.

ata Merge

¶ DATA MERGE USES SPREADSHEET DATA FOR CREATING "data publishing" documents like form letters, organizational charts, business cards, sequential stationery, project sheets, or any other type of data driven content. It uses a data source file whose content is merged into a target document. The data source file contains the information, *data-fields*, that will vary in each new instance of the target document, such as the names and addresses of the recipients of a form letter, or the names and photos of members in an organizational chart.

A data source like this data_fields.txt file produces a target document with variable content for each specific instance. Notice that the top row contains the data-fields.

Three data records are output to a single document page. Each record comprises fields for the dynamic data (name, rank, ID, and photo) and static elements that remain consistent (logo/header and photo frame). Paragraph styles are used to format the data-fields.

This is how the data record is set up on the source file for a multiple record layout. The record placement is fine-tuned in the Multiple Record Layout sub-panel within the Create Merged Document.

The data source file is made up of data-fields and records. *Fields* are for specific, changeable, information, such as names or postal codes, which are then grouped, oftentimes with static elements, into repeatable *records*. A data source file should be a comma delimited file (.csv) or a tab-delimited/semi-colon delimited file (.txt) in which each piece of data is separated by a tab or a semi-colon. These can be created in spreadsheet applications like Excel, Sheets, or Numbers and exported from there as CSV or TXT files.

The target document contains the data-field placeholders, which can contain both images and text, plus any other items that will remain the same in each instance of the merged document. By adding image data-fields to the data source file, you can allow a different image to appear on each merged record. For example, when you merge a document that includes information about various organization members, you can include an image of each member as part of the merge.

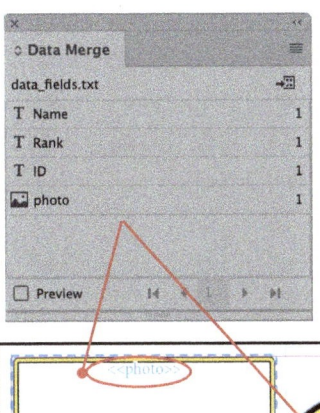

Use the Data Merge panel to create the data-fields by either dragging the field name from the Data Merge panel and dropping it into the appropriate frame on the document, or placing your cursor in that frame and double-clicking the field name in the panel. Remember, the data source file must be a CSV or TXT file.

The data-field placeholders on the source data record are identified by << >> surrounding them. They can be formatted with paragraph and object styles

All the elements in the layout are grouped to create the data record.

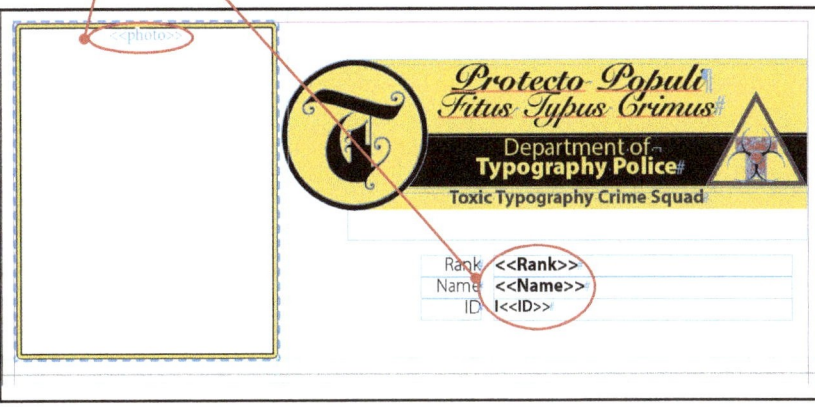

Use (@)photo for fields in the header row or first line of the data source file to place image files. If more than one image is to be placed, each one needs its own unique @photo linked path (@photo1, @photo2 etc.). The path to the placed files must follow the naming conventions of the operating system in which the image files are stored. Image files can only be stored on a server or a hard drive. URLs are ignored. These paths are case-sensitive. To use a path in the data source file, first place the image in its location. Select it in the Links panel and scroll through the Link Info section in the bottom of the panel to find its path. Right-click the path and choose "Copy…" with the path name you right-clicked on. Paste this into your data source file—the correct cell in your spreadsheet, or location in your text file. Repeat this for as many images there are. Save this source file in the correct CSV or TXT format and open it in the Data Merge panel. From there you can make the merged document containing all the records.

If you get an error message when you type the @ symbol at the beginning of the field, type an apostrophe (') before the @ symbol (like this '@photos) to validate the function. Some applications, such as Excel, require this since the @ symbol is reserved for its own functions.

The resulting merged document is a new InDesign document that contains the all information from the source document, repeated for as many instances there are of each record from the data source. The data record (the info you want to use) can be created on a document page or on the Parent page. Creating a merge from the Parent page maintains the link to the data source file (sometimes useful if the source needs to be updated), while making the merge on a document page breaks it. Sometimes it is easier to create a new data source file and import it, than to update an existing one. Depending on your needs you can choose to output a single record to a single page, or multiple records to a single page.

Steps for Merging Data

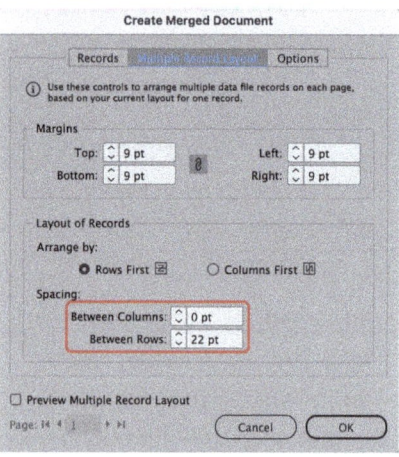

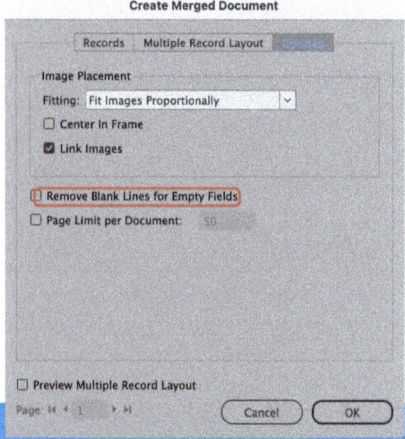

- ▶ Determine which data-fields you'll be using in your source and target documents. Design how you want the final document to look, so that you know which fields are necessary to accomplish the merge.
- ▶ Save the data source file—usually a spreadsheet or database file—as a comma-delimited (.csv) or tab- delimited (.txt) text file. Make sure that your data source file is structured in such a way that you can include the appropriate fields in your target document. For example, the top row of a spreadsheet should contain the field names that you'll use in the target document.
- ▶ Create a data record InDesign document that includes text and other items that remain the same in each version of the target document.
- ▶ Select the data source file (TXT or CSV) using the Data Merge panel.
- ▶ Insert fields from the Data Merge panel into the target document text frames. Put your cursor in the text frame, then double-click the appropriate field name in the Data Merge panel to insert it, or drag the field name into the text frame. These fields can be on a document page or a parent page but not both.
- ▶ Group all the elements that comprise the record.
- ▶ Preview the records using the Data Merge panel to make sure that the target document loads all the fields in the record. If a field fails to load it is most likely due to a punctuation error in the data source.
- ▶ When you choose Create Merged Document from the pull-down menu in the Data Merge panel, you can further fine-tune the positioning of the records on the page. Use the Multiple Record Layout sub-panel to adjust the positioning of the records.
- ▶ Merge the target document with the data source file to create the new InDesign document containing all the records.

If some of the data-fields do not have content, you can choose Remove Blank Lines For Empty Fields in the Options sub-panel of the Create Merged Document panel when merging the document to prevent empty lines. However, if any characters, including spaces, appear in the field for that line, the line is not removed.

Limitations for Data Merge

While any content in a spreadsheet cell or text file can be transformed into a styled element by Data Merge, remember that:

- Data Merge links to a data source—a CSV or TXT (tab-delimited or semicolon delimited) file only. Excel files (.xls or .xlsx) or database files are not recognized.
- Data Merge is not designed for long/complicated layouts. It works best with one record (a single row of spreadsheet content) per page/spread or one record per section of a page.
- You can only use one data source file per InDesign document.
- Data fields will only merge from a parent page/spread or document page/spread, not both.
- There is no support for if/then statements that might have been used in the spreadsheet.
- Data Merge does not recognize cell formats like currency, time, etc..
- Data Merge cannot flow text into multiple threaded text frames.
- There are also additional limitations associated with CSV files:
- You can't use merged cells
- You cannot insert a line break within a field in the data source file. If it's necessary to split a field across different lines, create two different fields, such as <<Address1>> and <<Address2>>.
- Row 1 of the spreadsheet must be the column headers
- For photos, the column header must start with @ symbol (i.e., @photo. Excel files require an apostrophe: '@photo)
- Photos must exist on a server or hard drive. URLs are not recognized. They are referenced either by image file name, or platform style path, depending on their location relative to the data file. You can find this path in the Links panel.

Long Documents and InDesign Books

¶ Any multi-page document that can be broken up into smaller more easily editable chunks, each its own file, may be considered a book. These could be chapters, articles, or sections of a larger work that may need to be edited. An InDesign Book file (.indb) allows for easy compilation, editing or reshuffling of the individual files that make up a book. It does not physically contain its component files, it only references them. If they were part of one continuous document, any editing or reshuffling would be an unwieldy task. Having the sections as separate documents that can be accessed from the book file makes editing and reordering much easier and more efficient, since you are working with smaller independent files: it is easier to edit and move any one file within the InDesign book than it is to cut and paste that section within a longer single document.

Some Guidelines for Constructing Flexible Long Documents

Avoid Multiples: Don't use multiple spaces, tabs or returns to create space within your document, use styles. This makes for cleaner documents and easier global editing. Need space between paragraphs? Make a style with a *Space After* or *Space Before*. Use a style with user defined tab stops to accurately position tabs.

Use as Few Frames as Possible: If you need a headline to cut across columns, use the *Span Columns* feature as a paragraph style, rather than a separate frame. This will automatically adapt to any edits as headlines are rewritten or changed in size without needing to manually modify the frame.

Minimize Overrides: Rather than deleting parent page items create a parent page that solves the problem. For example, if page numbers are obscured by an image, place them on higher layer, rather than cutting and pasting-in-place. Or if numbers need to be a different color in order to stand out against darker backgrounds, create a new parent page based on the original and make the changes there. Similarly, with any paragraph, character or object styles, if you're going to override more than one item, you're probably better of creating a new style for it. The fewer the overrides, the more flexibility you have for changes.

Minimize Forced Line Breaks: We often need to Force Line Breaks (Shift+ Return/Enter) to push text onto a new line within the same paragraph, but if you're doing it more than a few times perhaps you may need to turn hyphenation off or modify paragraph indents and spacing.

Use Indents or Insets Before Changing Frame Size: It's preferable to use indents (a text attribute) in a paragraph style or insets (a frame attribute) in an object style to change the position of text within a frame. This way, global edit can easily be applied.

Use a Template as a Starter File: Build a starter file with all the key attributes you want in your final document, and save it as a template. This file should contain all the things you need for each of the files that you will create for the project as a whole. This template should be so complete that if you were to send it to a collaborator to work on, their contribution would seemlessly integrate back into your project. At the very least, these are the attributes you should have in your template:

- ▶ Styles (Paragraph, Character, Object, Table, Cell, and Table of Contents)
- ▶ Swatches
- ▶ Parent Pages
- ▶ Layers (set up on parent pages)
- ▶ Preferences

Use InDesign's Book Feature to Control Long Documents: If the needs of the project are such that they will best be served by smaller documents, for example, breaks by chapters or sections, build it as an InDesign Book. The Book panel allows you to load any individual documents to make the book. It also allows you to sync items across all the documents by allowing you to set the *Style Source* document. By using *Synchronize Options* you can sync attributes globally in the book to the style source. Consider using a non-printing document with examples of all the used styles as the style source—very useful as a visual reference. This icon denotes the style source ⬚▸⬚. These attributes can be synced:

- ▶ Conditional Text Settings
- ▶ Numbered Lists
- ▶ Cross-reference Formats
- ▶ Text Variables
- ▶ Parent Pages
- ▶ Trap Presets
- ▶ Table Styles
- ▶ Cell Styles
- ▶ Object Styles
- ▶ TOC Styles
- ▶ Character Styles
- ▶ Paragraph Styles
- ▶ Swatches

For example, in a compilation of short stories each author's submission should be its own InDesign file. During production, some authors may update their submissions. The editor may also make changes to the order of the chapters. If this were a single document, it would be sisyphean nightmare of tediousness to make edits down the line. Having separate documents within the book structure alleviates most of these issues.

The initial ordering of the chapter files is easily modified within the Book panel by dragging them into the desired location. Pagination is automated. Items can also be synchronized to the file source ⬚▸⬚.

Name Swatches for Better Syncing with the Book Panel: By default, InDesign names swatches by their CMYK color values. Changing a swatch's values does not synchronize across a book's component documents, rather that new color is added to the each of the other document swatches. A workaround for this is to *name* the swatches. These names should be specific, like *title teal*, or *header red*, or even *color 1*. Syncing a named color swatch does update the color values throughout the book. Note that unsynced swatches are not deleted.

Open All Documents Before Syncing: While InDesign can sync unopened documents, having the documents open allows you to Undo and fix any mistakes that you might have made. Since it opens, syncs and saves changes in the background, you won't be able to Undo any errors if the documents were closed at the time of syncing.

Submitting the Book for Publication: It's common to submit your final InDesign file in PDF format, typically PDF/X-4. Find out from the printer if they want the PDF as single pages (most common) or spreads (less common), and if they require printers/crop marks. These can all be set in the PDF output options when exporting the file. Note that the cover is a separate file from the book contents, and it is roughly the spread size plus the thickness of the spine. Most printers will have a template or guidelines for this.

GREP

GREP IS A COMMAND-LINE UTILITY THAT SEARCHES plain-text datasets for matches to a regular expression, or pattern. It is part of InDesign's Find/Change query system. It's name is derived from the Unix command *g/re/p* (**g**lobal/ **r**egular expression search/and **p**rint). So what does it do? It is particularly useful for making changes in long documents.

By looking for patterns, it is possible to find strings of information that would be difficult to find with the typical Find/Change dialog, and make changes to them. Patterns, for example, like text within quotation marks, or phone numbers that use different conventions (hyphens between numbers, or brackets and hyphens, etc.) within the same document. GREP Styles can also be applied to text, for example, assigning a color to page numbers in a table of contents, or changing any text inside quote marks from regular to italics with a different text color, without changing the quote marks themselves.

In this example, creating a Table of Contents collects all the text in the original headline style, which includes the text styled in green. After a GREP search, the green text is deleted. A GREP style is applied to the page numbers.

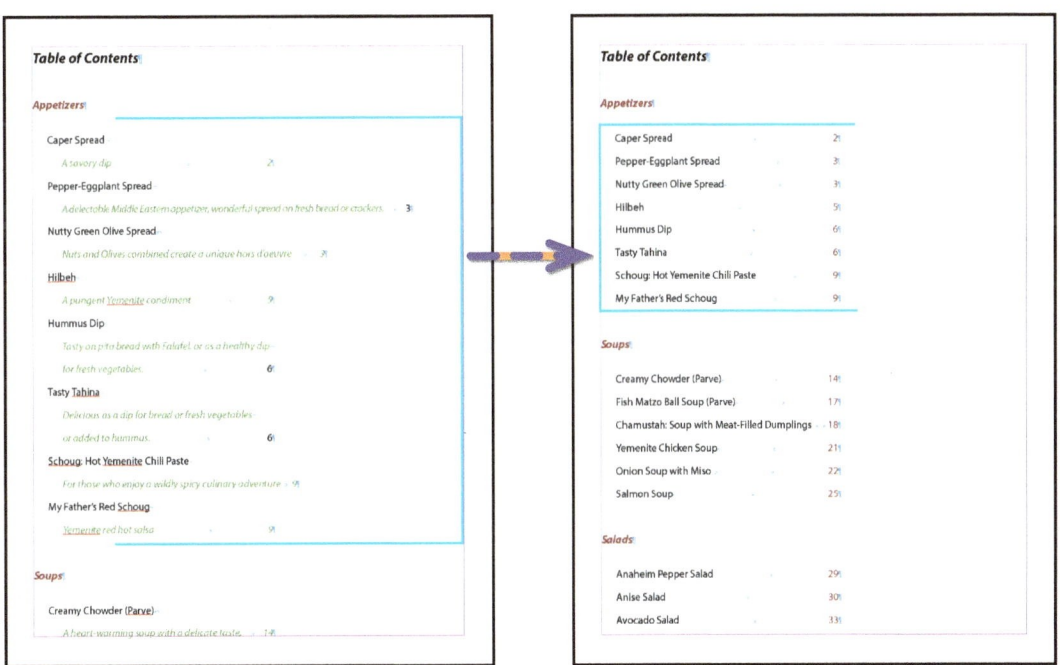

The headline style used in this cookbook example has the dish title on one line followed by its description on a new line, the green text, created by a soft return (forced line break). The tab space is automatically inserted when the TOC is created. In order to remove the unwanted line of text (the green text) a custom GREP query is used to find *any* text between a forced line break and a tab, and replace it with an empty space, effectively deleting it. An added bonus is that a significant amount of text space is also saved, reducing the amount of space the TOC would take up in the final document.

Get a GREP

If you feel like you've suddenly stumbled into a twilight zone of obscure practices and obtuse programming, fear not, you are not alone. Fortunately, some very smart people have done all the grunt work so you don't need reinvent the wheel, or more accurately, learn a programming language. Once you've used GREP, you'll look for other instances to use it. It's that powerful.

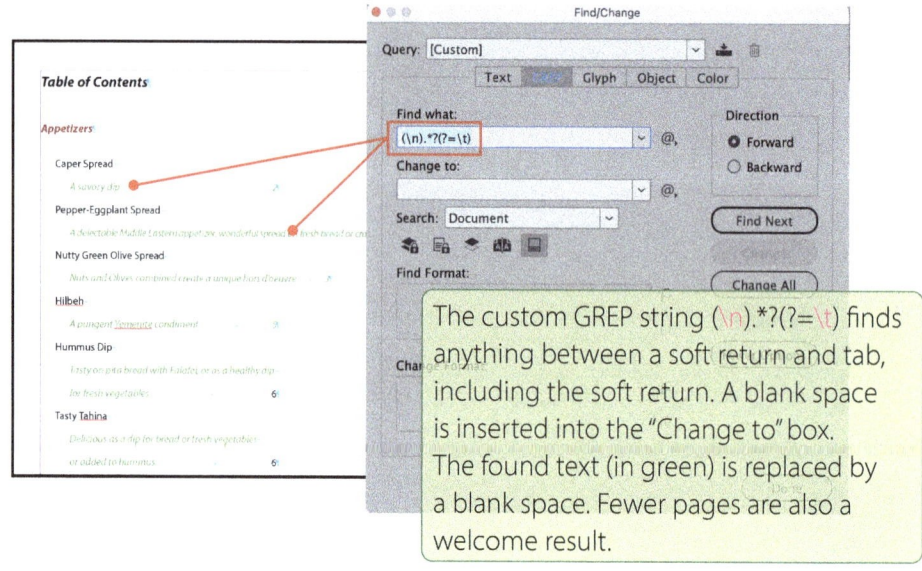

The custom GREP string (\n).*?(?=\t) finds anything between a soft return and tab, including the soft return. A blank space is inserted into the "Change to" box. The found text (in green) is replaced by a blank space. Fewer pages are also a welcome result.

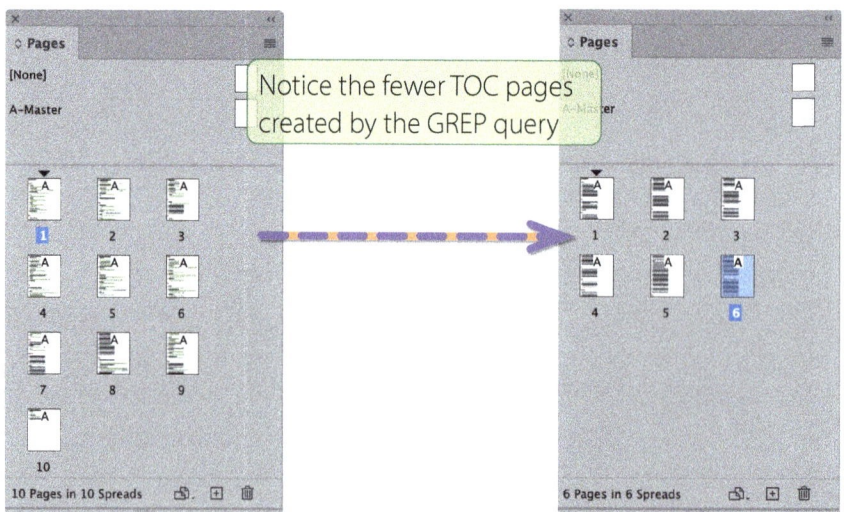

Notice the fewer TOC pages created by the GREP query

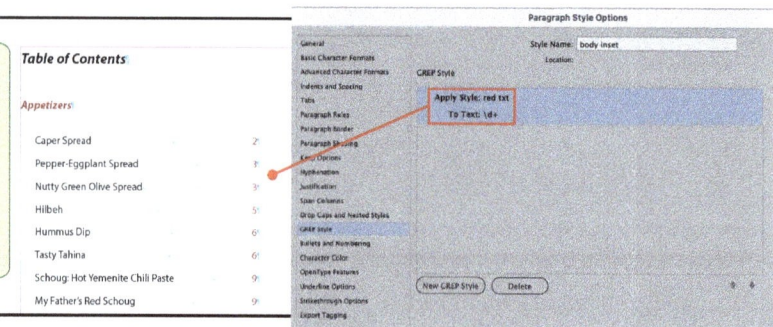

You can choose GREP Style to apply character style formatting to elements of your paragraph style (this one is called "body inset"). The style "red" is a character style that applies only to digits by using the GREP string \d+

Some Useful GREP Strings

These are some of the most common GREP usages. You can experiment with your own custom queries, and even find them online. Chances are, someone has needed or posted something similar to our needs. Any queries you may use, can be saved into InDesign, saving you from having to remember them, and saving you from potential self-inflected existential crises.

Finding "Or"

(Milk|Dark) Chocolate	Milk Chocolate or Dark Chocolate
(m|M)ilk (c|C)hocolate	Milk Chocolate, milk chocolate, milk Chocolate, Milk chocolate
[mM]ilk chocolate	milk chocolate or Milk chocolate
[^m]ilk	ailk, bilk, cilk, etc., but not milk
(?i)milk	Case insensitive: Milk, milk, mILk, etc.
colou?r	color or colour (the ? means the previous character or expression may or may not be there)

Wildcards

[cC][\l\u]+e	Any string of letters that starts with "c" and ends with "e", such as chocolate, Chocolate, care, case, coarse, etc.
\<c\w+e\>	Any whole word that begins with "c" and ends with "e"
\bc\w+e\b	Exactly the same as above, but using \b for "word boundary"
\s+$	All spaces at the end of a paragraph
\s+\Z	Remove spaces at end of story
[\l\u\d.]+@[\l\u\d.]+	Simple e-mail address (e.g. dingbat@typopo.com or dd@DTP.net)
\d{4}	Find any four digits (the curly brace expression is not found in the InDesign @ menu)
[-\u\l\d._]+@[-\u\l\d_]+\.[\u\l]{2,4}	More "robust" email (e.g. dana-dingbat_1@typopopo.com)
\d+/\d+	Any fraction, such as 1/2, 22/7, or 355/113
(?<!\d)(?<!/)\d+/(?!11)(?!0)(?!9)\d{1,3}(?!/)(?!\d)	Robust fraction grep: Will find fractions, but leave out dates such as 6/98, 9/11, or 6/17/2012. Unfortunately, it fails on 355/113 (which happens to be a reasonably good approximation of π, proving that nothing is perfect).
[[=a=]]	Find any kind of "a", no matter the accent, including a, á, à, ä, etc.
(?<=\d)(rd|th|st)	Find st, rd, or th ordinals (such as 1st, 2nd, 3rd) that follow a digit—in order to apply superscript to just the ordinal (not the digit).
(?<=\().+?(?=\))	Find any text inside parentheses, but not including the parentheses. This uses "Positive Lookbehind" and "Positive Lookahead"

To search for a character that has symbolic meaning in GREP, enter a backslash \ before the character to "escape" it. This indicates that the character that follows is literal. For example, a period . searches for any character in a GREP search; to search for an actual period, enter \.

Escape

\$\d\.\d\d	Find a dollar sign followed by one digit, a period, and two digits. Note that the dollar and dot have to be "escaped" because they mean something different in GREP.
\(.+\)	Find anything inside parentheses (again, parentheses need to be escaped)
\Q(a+b*c?)\E	Escape everything; that is, find (a+b*c) exactly, without having to worry about escaping each special character.

Useful Tricks

DESCRIPTION	FIND	CHANGE TO
Add an anchored object at the beginning of each paragraph (cut object to clipboard first)	^(.)	~C$1
Reverse first and last name (but watch out for middle names or initials, too)	^(\w+)([.\w]+)? (\w+)	$3, $1$2
After reversing the names (see above), fix any last names that started with Van or De.	^(\w+, [.\w]+) (Van|De)	$2 $1
Find and remove duplicate words	\b(\w+)\b \1	$1
Find and remove duplicate paragraphs/lines in a list	^(.+\r)\1+	$1
Find lists in which people have actually typed a number followed by a period followed by a space, and apply automatic numbered list style.	^\d+\. ?(.)	$1 (and apply paragraph style that includes auto numbers)

Use parentheses to divide your search into *subexpressions*. For example, if you want to search for "cat" or "cot," you can use the c(a|o)t string. Parentheses are especially useful to identify groupings. For example, searching for "the (cat) and the (dog)" identifies "cat" as Found Text 1 and "dog" as Found Text 2. You can use the Found Text expressions (such as $1 for Found Text 1) to change only that part of the found text. Found Text refers to the text within the parentheses, the subexpression.

Finding Text Within Quotation Marks

Suppose you want to search for any word enclosed in quotation marks (such as "Spain"), and you want to remove the quotation marks and apply a style to the word (so that it becomes *Spain* instead of Spain). The expression (")(\w+) (") includes three groupings, as indicated by parentheses ( ). The first and third groupings search for any quotation mark, and the second grouping searches for one or more word characters.

You can use the Found Text expressions to refer to these groupings. For example, $0 refers to all found text, and $2 refers to only the second grouping.

By inserting $2 in the Change To field and specifying a character style in the Change Format field, you can search for a word within quotation marks, and then replace the word with a character style. Because only $2 is specified, the $1 and $3 groupings are removed. (Specifying $0 or $1$2$3 in the Change To field would apply the character style to the quotation marks as well.)

This example searches only for single words enclosed in quotation marks. If you want to search for phrases enclosed in parentheses, add wildcard expressions, such as (\s*.*\w*\d*), which looks for spaces, characters, word characters, and digits.

Find and Change Phone Numbers

InDesign includes a number of search presets that you can choose from the Queries menu. For example, you can choose the Phone Number Conversion query, which looks like this:

\(?(\d\d\d)\)?[-.]?(\d\d\d)[-.]?(\d\d\d\d)

Phone numbers in the United States can appear in a variety of formats, such as 323-555-3982, (323) 555-3982, 323.555.3982, and 323 555 3982. This string looks for any of these variations. The first three digits (\d\d\d) of the phone number may or may not be enclosed in parentheses, so a question mark appears before and after the parentheses: \(? and \)?. Note that the backslash \ indicates that the actual parenthesis is being searched for and that it's not part of a subexpression. The brackets [ ] locate any character within them, so in this case, [-.] finds either a hyphen, a period, or a space. The question mark after the brackets indicates that the items within it are optional in the search. Finally, the digits are enclosed in parentheses, which signify groupings that can be referred to in the Change To field.

You can edit the grouping references in the Change To field to suit your needs. For example, you could use these expressions:

$1.$2.$3 = 323.555.3982
$1–$2–$3 = 323–555–3982
($1) $2–$3 = (323) 555–3982
$1 $2 $3 = 323 555 3982

To Find 'between'

?<= finds anything, but not including the instance specified. For example, find [some text] that's in between [whatever], and then apply formatting to just the text, not what's surrounding it. One example would be formatting parenthetical text without formatting the parentheses themselves: turn (this) into (*this*) and (that other thing) into (*that other thing*) all at once, throughout the story or document, with a simple click.

Here's the GREP expression that finds one or more words of parenthetical content, but doesn't include the parentheses themselves in the found instances:

(?<=\().*?(?=\))

If you copy and paste that GREP string into the Find What field in the Edit > Find/Change > GREP panel of InDesign, and then click the Find Next button, InDesign selects the first instance of parenthetical text, but not the parentheses themselves. You can also change just the found text's formatting by specifying what you want in the Change Format area (leave the Change To and Find Format text fields blank).

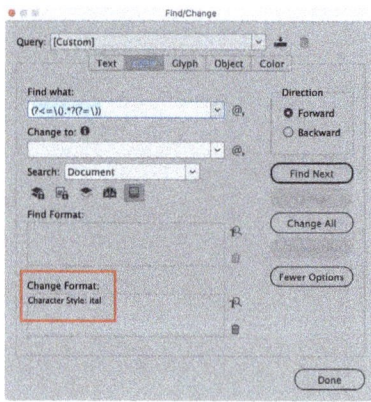

Modify the Search

Changing the characters highlighted in red allows you to find other "surrounding items" like quote marks or em dashes. The first instance is an opening parenthesis, which needs to be "escaped" with a backslash so InDesign knows it's a literal parenthesis, not some more GREP code. The second instance is the closing parenthesis, again preceded by a backslash to escape it.

(?<=\().*?(?=\))

So, to find text surrounded by a pair of em dashes (but not the em dashes themselves) you'd change both instances of the red characters so it finds an em dash instead of an opening or closing parenthesis. You can type these em dashes into the Find field, but not all keyboards access those optional or hidden characters in the same way. Sometimes it's simpler to let InDesign get the characters that the GREP code needs.

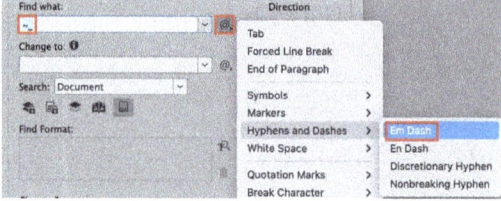

Choose the special character you want from the dropdown menu with an atsign (@) next to the GREP Find What field. According to the dropdown menu, GREPese for an em dash is a tilde followed by an underscore ~_. Copy this code and replace the parenthesis code with it. The string to find text in between em-dashes is:

(?<=~_).*?(?=~_)

Similarly, his string finds text in between any double quotes:

(?<=").*?(?=")

This type of GREP search is called a *Lookaround* — a combination of a Lookahead and a Lookbehind. All the "look" types of GREP searches share one thing in common, they let you find some text based on a character that precedes or follows it, but not to include that character in the found text itself.

Save the GREP String

If you find any custom GREP string to be useful, click the save query icon in the GREP panel of Find/Change so you can save it and recall it from the dropdown menu of saved searches at any later time. This menu list shows only the GREP string, not what it does, so you may also find it useful to make a list of the GREPs you use or may want to use. This is a great timesaver if you are not a coder and have no interest in being one, but want the occasional power of GREP without having to memorize what the characters symbolize.

Some Useful Tips

Quick Apply

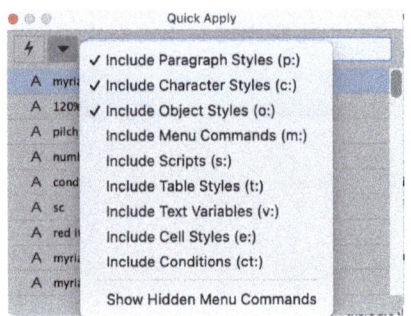

This handy little panel really speeds up formatting, especially locally—it's the lightning bolt symbol on the character/paragraph styles panels and the control bar—and can be accessed by hitting cmd/ctrl + return. Any attribute that has previously been saved as style can be applied from it. For example, the magenta text in this paragraph is created by first selecting it, hitting cmd/ctrl + return, and then clicking on the relevant character style in the Quick Apply panel. By default, the panel lists all the style options available, but you can filter it down to those styles you use most, like Character, Paragraph and perhaps Object.

Footnotes and Endnotes

Academic and research texts often use footnotes or endnotes. A *footnote* has two linked parts: its reference number that appears in the text, and the footnote itself that appears at the bottom of the column or page it is referenced on. Footnotes and endnotes are numbered automatically. *Endnotes* appear at the end of their chapter or section. InDesign is able to create them or honor them in imported text. Typically, you'd get a Word or RTF document that has these references and you'd use InDesign to style them according to the publishers' guidelines. Formatting styles are determined by the publisher and usually follow MLA, CMS, or APA guidelines. If you do need to insert them manually, InDesign has the tools to do so under the Type menu. Remember that any text using footnotes implies that there will also be a bibliography listing the citations. Bibliographies should appear at the end of the document. They are quite easily formatted with nested styles. *Italics* are always used for titles:

> Cruxley, Aldus, *The Road to Dystypia*, San Francisco, Peripheral Press, 2024
> Dingbat, Darius, *Crimes Against Typography*, Los Angeles, DTP Press, 2024
> Mayvell, Reeves, *Gorilla Type*, New York, Perdido Street Press, 2020

Bibliographies are styled according to guidelines typically set by MLA, CMS, or APA. Titles are always *italicized*.

Footnote and Endnote related commands are found under the Type menu

Insert Footnote
Document Footnote Options...
Insert Endnote
Document Endnote Options...
Convert Footnotes and Endnotes...

Footnotes (blue text below the horizontal rule) and their reference number (red number) can be styled. The footnote number size is determined by the superscript setting in the Preferences panel. The first footnote entry contains the complete bibliographic entry, Subsequent entries of the same source cite just the author and the page number, and are an additional paragraph style.

Are any crimes against typography waranted? Dingbat argues that … blah blah blah and hokum pokum with lot's of gum-beating.[1] Cruxley counters that … blah blah and more blah blah is inevetible.[2] However, there does seem to be … hokum pokum blah blah that overlaps perspectives. Take, for instance, the dark AI that … blah and blah and even hokum with some more pokum. While Dingbat is not very clear on this, it may be inferred that… hokum pokum with blah.[3] Of course, that is not the position that Cruxley advocates, but neither is it … blah hokum blah pokum.[4]

1. Dingbat, Darius, *Crimes Against Typography* (Los Angeles: DTP Press, 2024), 37.
2. Cruxley, Aldus, *The Road to Dystypia* (San Francisco: Peripheral Press, 2024), 43.
3. Dingbat, *Crimes Against Typography*, 72–3
4. Cruxley, *The Road to Dystypia*, 68

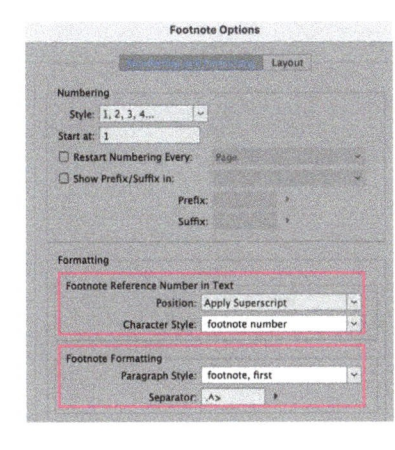
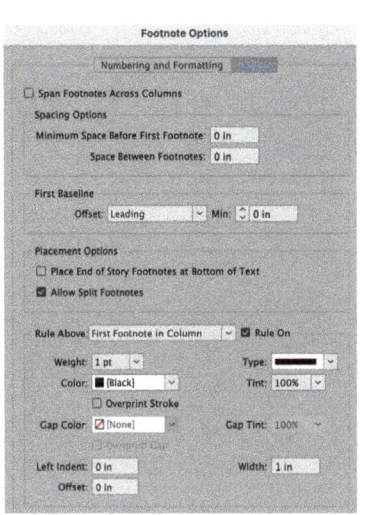

Glyphs and Special Characters

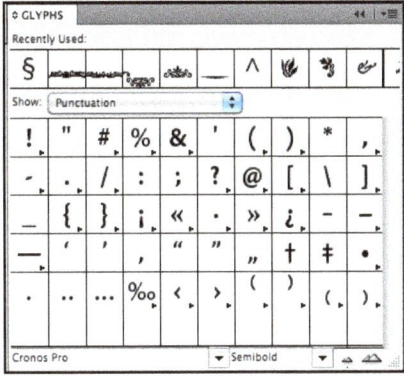

Glyphs, or specific forms of characters, are accessed via the Glyphs panel. Initially this panel shows glyphs for the font where the cursor is located, but any font can be viewed. Many fonts, especially OpenType fonts, will often have multiple variations for standard characters. These and any of the special characters found in the Glyphs panel can be inserted into the text: place the cursor at the insertion point in the text, and then double-click the character in the Glyphs panel to insert it. The triangle icons in the lower right corners of the character boxes indicate that there are alternates available for the characters. Glyphs can also be filtered by using the Show pull-down menu. The Glyphs panel is especially useful for inserting ornamental characters:

Shaping Text Frames

By reshaping text frames you are able to add interest to blocks of text. Use the Direct Selection Tool to select the individual corner points of a frame in order to move them. Holding the option key with the Pen Tool allows you to convert corner points and add curves. In order to manipulate the points you draw, hold down the cmd/ctrl key to access the Selection Tool. Otherwise you will just be adding points or continuing a line.

The Pen Tool has an interactive cursor that informs you about its intent in its relation to anchor points—there are tiny icons to the right of the pen cursor that show up. This is what they mean:

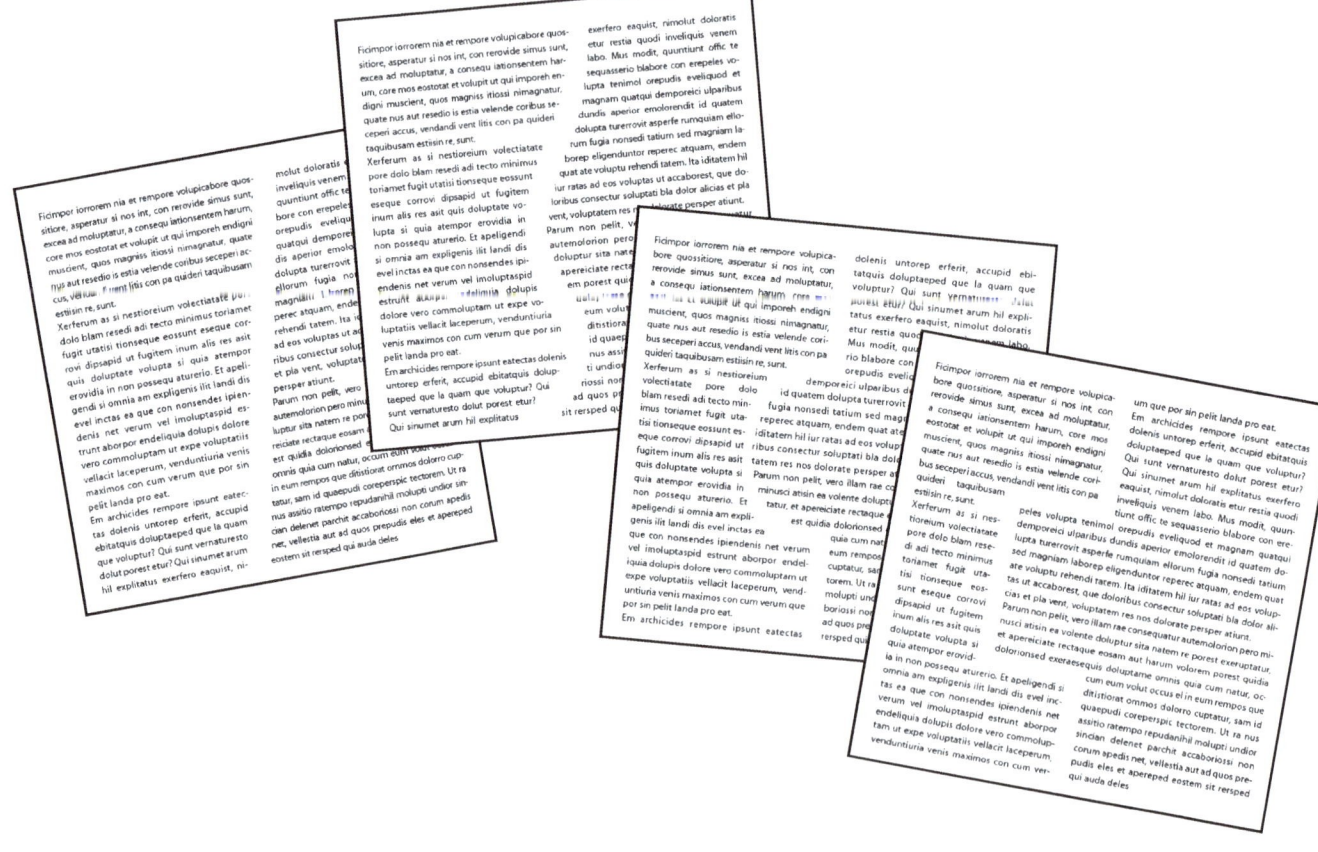

- x you are ready to set the starting point (it disappears once you have done this)
- + will add an anchor point to an existing line segment (anywhere between two adjacent anchor points)
- − will remove an anchor point when you click on it
- ^ will extend control handles when you click-and-drag on an anchor point (to make curves)
- o will close a path (shape) when you click on the end point
- / activates an endpoint, allowing you to continue drawing

Alternate Layouts and Liquid Layout Rules

Using *Liquid Layout* rules, objects can be adjusted to the changed layout. Different pages can use different liquid rules, but only one rule can be used per page You can streamline the process of creating and maintaining two or more layouts with the same content using Alternate Layouts (Layout > Create Alternate Layout…). While it is not a perfect solution, it speeds up the process of reformatting completed documents to different dimensions, and to some extent different orientations. Changing orientation will require more tweaking to fit the layout than keeping the same orientation but with different dimensions. The alternate layouts are displayed in the pages panel.

> Using liquid rules when resizing documents in the same orientation can minimize the need for layout adjustment or tweaking.

> Adapting vertical layouts to horizontal ones does require adjustments. Preserving the existing liquid rules places content off the page and on the pasteboard. Scaling the content fits it to the new page, while maintaining the aspect ratio.

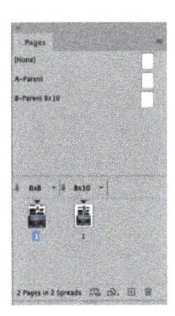

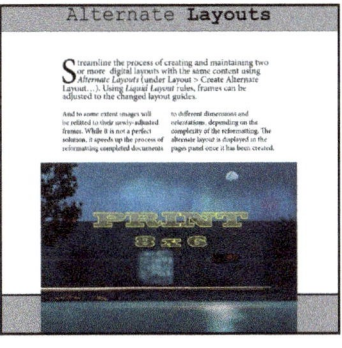
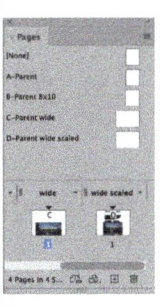
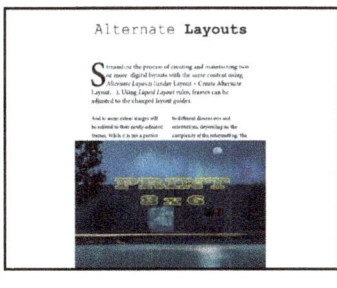

Liquid page rules can be applied from the Layout menu (Layout > Liquid Layout) or by using the Page tool. Click a page with the Page tool and then choose a liquid page rule from the control bar. You can change page size with the Page tool, but using a mouse to do so is not as accurate as using the width and height widgets in the control bar.

> Note: If you don't need multiple layouts, you can just change the document size, using liquid layout rules as needed, to control the resizing.

Jump Lines

Jump lines, "continued on" and "continued from," are used to track threaded text as it jumps between text frames. For example, text on a page might need to jump to another page that does not immediately follow it. This is a fairly common practice in magazine layout, as in "continued on page 36" and "continued from page 27." Jump lines are easily made by using special characters called markers. These are put into their own text frames touching or overlapping the threaded text frames. Make and position a text frame, type the text you want to appear before the number, and then insert the marker. Typically, the "continued on" text marker frame is positioned at the bottom of the threaded frame where the text ends, and the "continued from" marker frame is above the frame that the text jumps to. (Type > Insert Special Character > Markers > Next Page Number or Previous Page Number). Use "Next Page Number" on the page you are jumping from, and "Previous Page Number" on the page you have jumped to (*an example of this* is on pages 48 and 49). Jump lines will update accordingly if the page order changes.

The text frames with the Next/ Previous Page Number marker should touch or overlap the main text frame on the page for the numbers to appear correctly. If they don't touch, the page number that they are on will display.

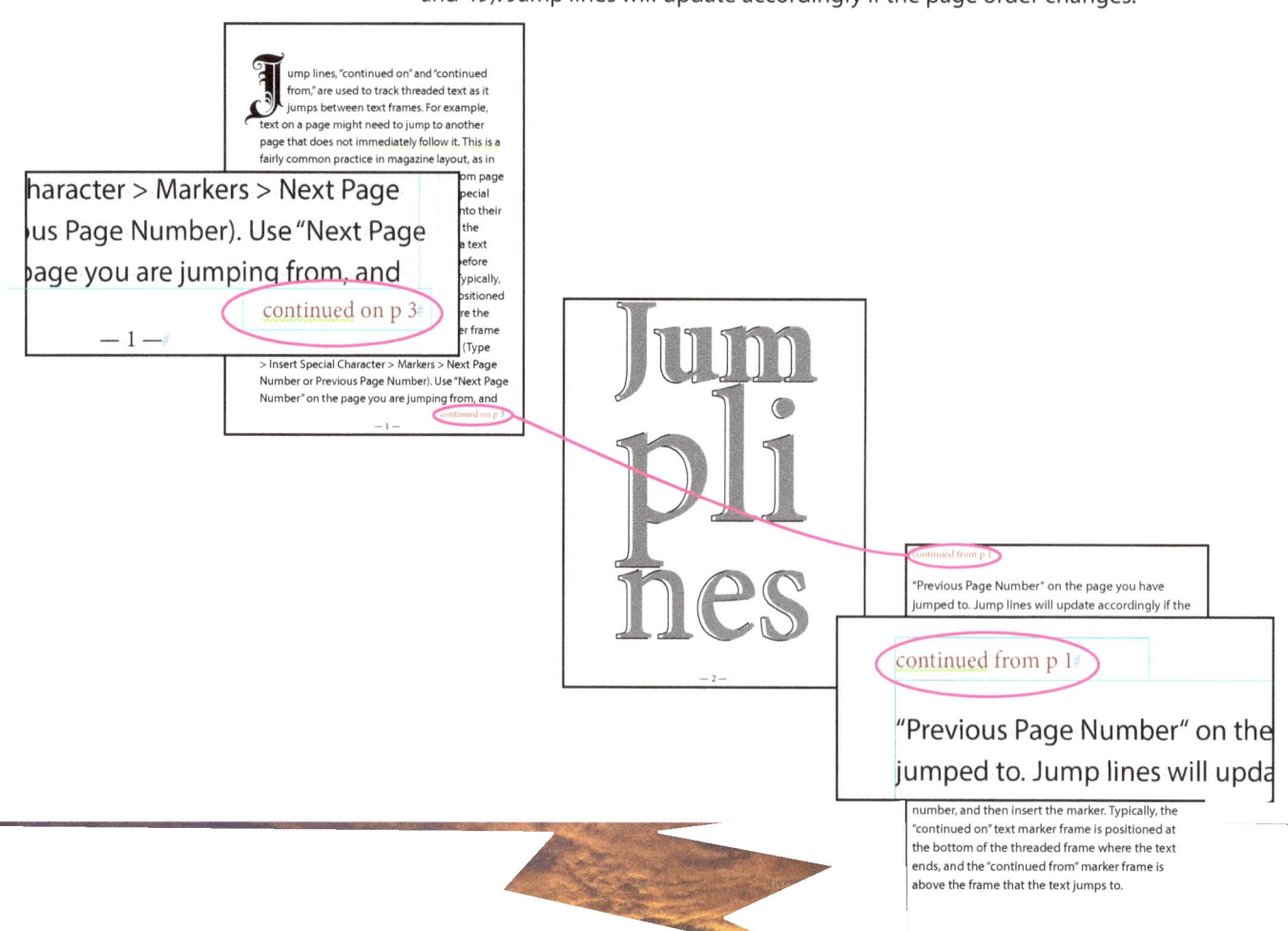

Story Editor and Copy Editor

You can use Story Editor (Edit > Edit in Story Editor, cmd/ctrl + Y) to edit text in InDesign without the distraction of formatting. The appearance—typeface, size and spacing—you choose to use in the story editor (specified in Preferences) does not affect the formatting of the document, it is for editing only. Any text edits, including styles and formatting, will be reflected in the layout window. It is also where you can view text that has been added, removed, or edited if *track changes* has been turned on. Since stories appear in their own story editor window, this window can be very useful for checking how much overset text there is.

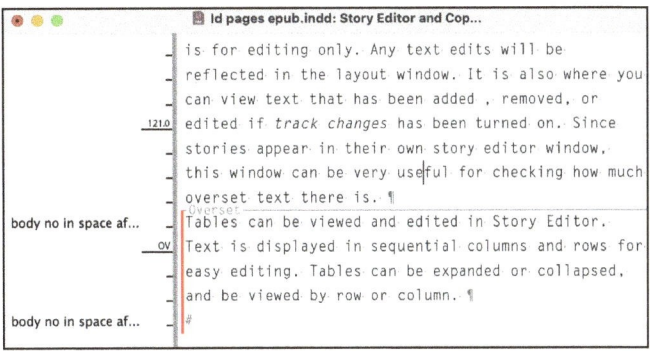

The Story Editor shows the paragraph styles used, which can be applied from within it, and any overset text there may be. It also represents, using icons, attributes and objects within the story that may not be displayed, like inline (anchored) objects, hyperlinks, variables etc.

Tables can be viewed and edited in Story Editor. Text is displayed in sequential columns and rows for easy editing. Tables can be expanded or collapsed, and viewed by row or column by right clicking in the panel.

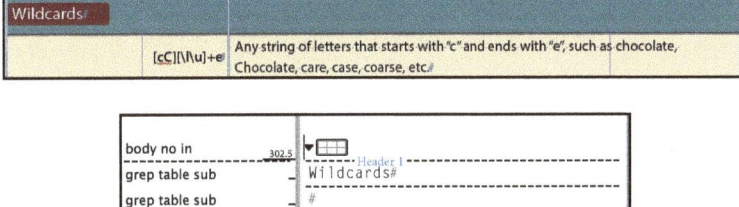

A table row and how it appears in the story editor

Multiple stories can be opened at the same time. Note that with long stories there is often a lag when typing or editing the text since the whole story is "live." Using the Copy Editor (Edit > Edit in Copy Editor (Beta), option/alt + shift + Y) avoids this issue and is an alternative when needing to do a lot of typing quickly. Copy Editor opens a new window that does not update live to the layout. Nor does it support text formatting and styles. Click the *Done* button in its window to set the changes once you have finished, to return to the layout. This is a Beta feature, only available for limited geographical locations and users, that will be implemented in future updates of InDesign.

Linking and Duplicating Content

The Content Collector tool is useful for reusing, managing and linking page items within and across documents. Use it to duplicate page items and place them across open InDesign documents. The Content Conveyor, which opens automatically when one of the Content tools is selected, displays the collected content for easy placement.

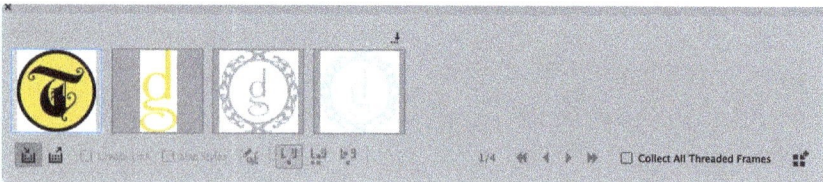

Selecting the object you want to collect with the Content Collector tool automatically places it in the Content Conveyor. Pressing B on the keyboard toggles between the Content Collector and Content Placer tools. Click in your document where you want the item to be placed.

Copying and Applying Text or Object Attributes

You can quickly copy text and object attributes, styles, even transformations, with the Eyedropper tool. Click on the text or object whose style you wish to copy. The Eyedropper will flip its orientation and appear to be filled. Click on the text or object you want to apply the copy to. If your object or text is already selected, using the tool will automatically apply the formatting or color from the text or object you click on. Double clicking on the tool allows you to customize its settings.

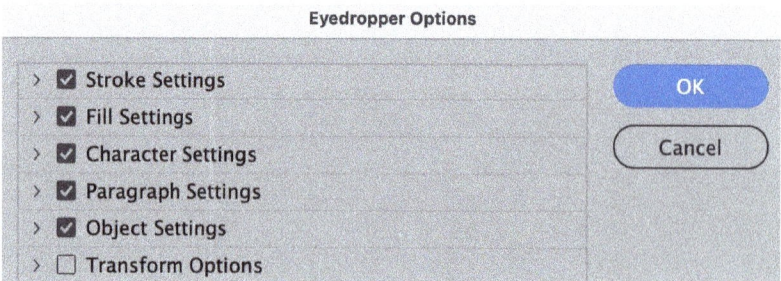

You can also copy a color or create a theme from colors in a photo or graphic, by using the Color Theme eyedropper.

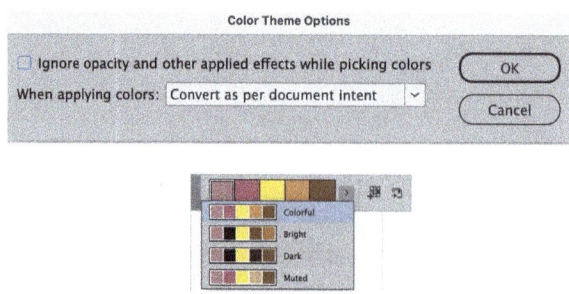

Fitting Objects to Frames

The Object > Fitting commands can be used to fit a frame and its content if they are of different sizes. To streamline this fitting, you can set General Preferences (cmd/ctrl + K) to enable *Content-Aware Fit* as the default.

The image is placed, with **Content Aware Fill** off.

The image is placed, with **Content Aware Fill** on. This fitting is similar to **Fill Frame Proportionally.**

Fit Frame To Content.

Fit Content Proportionally.

Fit Content To Frame. Note the image distortion—it has been squashed to fit the frame.

Frame Fitting

Fill Frame Proportionally: Resizes content to fill the entire frame while preserving the content's proportions.

Fit Content Proportionally: Resizes content to fit a frame while preserving the content proportions.

Content-Aware Fit: Automatically fits an image inside the frame based on the image content and frame size. Go to Preferences > General and select Make Content-Aware Fit the default frame fitting option to make this the default frame-fitting option.

Fit Frame To Content: Resizes the frame to fit the content.

Fit Content To Frame: Resizes content to fit the frame.

Center Content: Centers content within a frame.

Clear Frame Fitting Options: Removes undesired fitting settings applied with Auto-Fit.

You are able to see if there is any content outside the bounds of the frame. Using the Selection tool, hover over the image in the frame. A semi-transparent target appears on the image to signify that it is able to be selected. Clicking the target will show the image boundary as a thin brownish frame; pressing the target will reveal the hidden/masked areas as a screened image, very useful for positioning an image within the crop of a frame.

Clicking the target reveals the bounds of the image.

Pressing the target reveals the image and allows it to be moved around.

Interactive Documents

¶ INDESIGN CAN CREATE MANY KINDS OF INTERACTIVE document types, such as "e-zines," fixed-layout and reflowable EPUBs, and interactive flyers or brochures originally intended for print, by adding interactive elements to them. These could be buttons, forms, animations, videos, and sounds. Animation effects, like animated logos, are created using the Animation panel. Movies (H.264-encoded formats like MP4) and sounds (MP3 files) can be placed in your document, and are controlled in the Media panel. The Buttons and Forms panel is used to insert form fields and interactive buttons into your documents. Additional navigation is controlled by using hyperlinks. Document setup is determined by its *intent*, typically Web or Mobile.

The Export dialog offers two PDF options, *print* and *interactive*, and two EPUB options, *fixed* or *reflowable*. The Adobe PDF (Print) format supports minimal interactivity. Intended primarily for printing, hyperlinking to email and websites is supported in the digital file. The Adobe PDF (Interactive) format supports most kinds of interactivity, including animation, sound, and video, and is intended for onscreen viewing. The EPUB format also supports interactivity. Reflowable EPUBS are best suited for text-based documents, like novels, while fixed layout EPUBS are used for text or recipe books, and magazine-style layouts.

Choose File > Publish Online to publish any InDesign document to the web and share it on social networks, over email, or as a standalone URL. The online document supports all of InDesign's interactivity.

> Mobile and Web settings use pixels as units. Note that you will need to increase your type settings by 150–350 percent to compensate for the relative scaling of mobile documents due to device resolution. For example, a print-oriented page using 10pt type might need 30pt type for it to appear similar for viewing on a high resolution tablet. A "page" on an IPad Retina display is set up as 1536 x 2048 pixels, (21.33 x 28.44 inches), or about 270% bigger than the print page.

Hyperlinks

Hyperlinks can be created to pages, text anchors, email addresses, URLs, and files. These links are viewed or selected when the InDesign file is exported to Adobe PDF or Interactive PDF, EPUB, or HTML. A hyperlink source can be text, a text frame, or graphics frame. A hyperlink destination can be a URL, file, email address, page text anchor, or shared destination that opens when selecting the hyperlink. Sources can only jump to one destination, but many sources can jump to the same destination. (Type > Hyperlinks and Cross References > New Hyperlink).

External destinations are typically on servers or other sites, while internal destinations are within the same document. Shared hyperlink destinations are listed in the Hyperlinks panel (Window > Interactive > Hyperlinks). You can use any valid Internet resource protocol like http://, file://, ftp://, or mailto://, to hyperlink to external locations. InDesign can automatically convert any of these internet resource protocols in an open document to an active hyperlink (Type > Hyperlinks & Cross-References > Convert URLs to Hyperlinks…). The Hyperlinks panel will display a green dot next to the URL if it is valid, assuming you have an active internet connection.

> Hyperlinks can be used to open email to send a message, open an external website or a file on a website, and navigate to sections within a document.

Hyperlink to an External Location		
URL	File	Email
Link To: Select URL from the drop-down.	**Link To**: Select File from the drop-down.	**Link To**: Select Email from the drop-down.
Destination: Enter the URL.	**Path**: Enter the file location.	**Address**: Enter the email address.
You can also use Buttons to link to web pages.		**Subject Line**: Enter the subject for the email.

Text hyperlinks can have character styles applied to them (InDesign does have its own default Hyperlink character style which you can edit). Note that InDesign will apply its default Hyperlink appearance (blue underlined text) to any URL text it converts. This should be edited to fit your design since the Department of Typography Police are quite fussy about underlined text, which is a throw-back to mechanical typewriter days. Typewriters only had one monospaced typeface, and underlining text was the only way to imply emphasis or italics. Some typography police consider underlined text to be a crime against typography[1].

Hyperlink to an Internal Location		
Page	Text Anchor	Shared Destination
Document: Select the document from the drop-down..	**Document**: Select the document from the drop-down.	**Document**: Select the document from the drop-down.
Page: Enter the page number.	**Text Anchor**: Select an anchor from the drop-down.	**Address**: Enter the email address.
Zoom Setting: Select from Fixed, Fit View, Fit in Window, Fit Width, Fit Height, Fit Visible, or Inherit Zoom. You can also use buttons to link to web pages.		**Name**: Select an anchor or any saved URL, file, or email from the drop-down.

To create a text hyperlink, insert the text cursor at the beginning of the paragraph or text you want to link to. Choose New Hyperlink Destination from the drop-down in the Hyperlinks panel. Then choose Text Anchor from the Link To drop-down menu and name it appropriately. Using text anchors is often preferable to using page numbers, especially if the text location might change to a different page due to editing.

---

1 In a digital edition, this gratuitous footnote could contain a hyperlink to the section on Crimes Against Typography

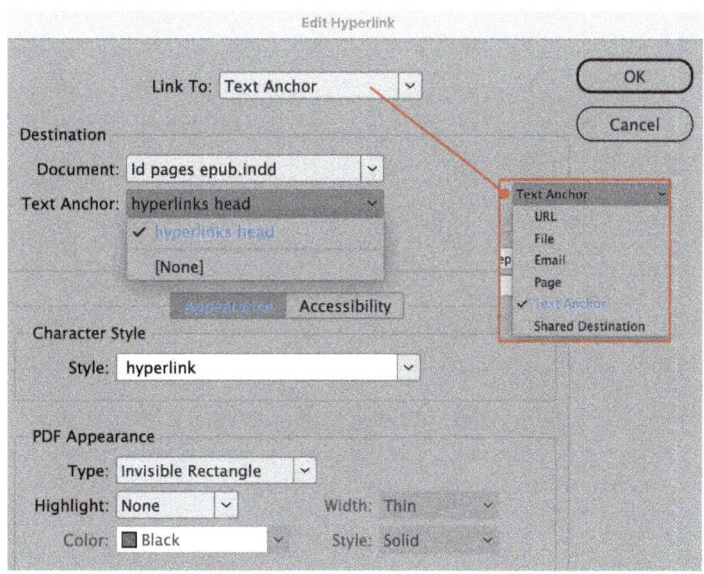

You can target different destinations with hyperlinks. The link here uses a text anchor, named **hyperlinks head** to jump to a text anchor that has been inserted at the section's heading.

Converting email or web addresses to hyperlinks is particularly useful for PDF documents like resumes that may link to portfolio sites, email and social media. You can find, convert and style URLs within your InDesign document: (Type > Hyperlinks and Cross References > Convert URLs to Hyperlinks…).

As an example of an internal destination, this hyperlink in a digital edition could take you to the beginning of the *Hyperlinks* section if clicked. Note that external hyperlinks require an internet connection.

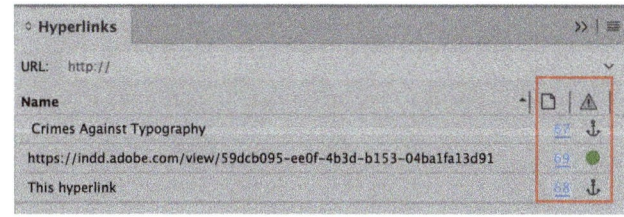

The Hyperlinks panel shows the type and status of the hyperlinks.

Making an MSO Button

This example uses two MSO buttons. When one button is clicked, its appearance changes to its "off" state, and the other button's appearance is turned "on." Other actions, like targeting slideshows or other MSOs, can also be added.

▶ Align the two objects that will be the MSO states on top of each other, and convert them to a multi-state object by clicking the + in the bottom of in the Object States panel. Name this MSO 1.
▶ Draw an empty rectangle to cover the MSO. Keep it selected and convert it to a button using the Buttons and Forms panel. This "invisible" button will target the MSO states and trigger other actions.
▶ Group the invisible button with the MSO.
▶ Repeat this process to make a second MSO.

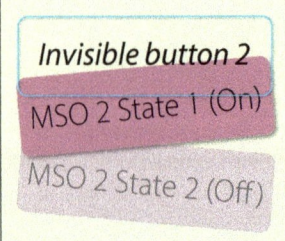

Buttons

To view this section published online, use this link:
https://indd.adobe.com/view/59dcb095-ee0f-4b3d-b153-04ba1fa13d91

¶ BUTTONS CAN PERFORM ACTIONS WHEN THE DOCUMENT is exported as a fixed layout EPUB or Interactive PDF. For example, a button can jump to a different page, open a website, or click through a slideshow. Buttons can be made from any object, drawn shape, or dragged into the document from the Sample Buttons and Forms panel. They can also have *appearances* or states, such as on/off/hover. The Buttons and Forms panel is used to make the buttons interactive. Multi-state objects can also act as buttons—an invisible button attached to the MSO can target its states and trigger actions, making it appear as if the MSO is interactive.

▶ When clicked or tapped,
Invisible button 1 targets MSO 1 State 2 (off), and MSO 2 State 1 (on). It also targets the corresponding state of the hidden "is active" text MSO that appears below MSO 1.
▶ When clicked or tapped,
Invisible button 2 targets MSO 2 State 2 (off), and MSO 1 State 1(on). It also targets the corresponding state of the hidden "is active" text MSO that appears below MSO 2.

When a button is active, its *off* state is visible. The other (inactive) button's *on* state is visible, implying that it is ready to be clicked. The invisible button (blue dashed line) on top of MSO 1 targets the *off* state of MSO 1, while simultaneously targeting the *on* state of MSO 2. Note that the related "is active" text is another targeted MSO, positioned below the two buttons. The invisible button on top of MSO 2 similarly targets the on/off states of the buttons and the related "is active" state of the third MSO.

MSO 1 State 1 (On)   MSO 2 State 1 (On)

*Buttons are dormant until clicked.
Clicking activates the buttons as shown below*

MSO 1 State 2 Off   MSO 2 State 1 On

MSO 1 is active

MSO 1 State 1 On   MSO 2 State 2 Off

MSO 2 is active

The MSO with the "is active" text has three states: text related to each active state and an empty frame with no text that is only active when both buttons are clickable.

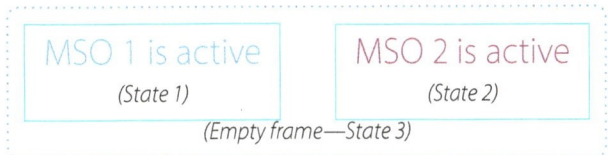

Slideshows

¶ A SLIDESHOW IS AN EPUB AND PUBLISH Online feature that allows for a series of image files to be displayed without them being on separate pages. A multistate object (MSO) is used where each slide is a different state of the object, so a 10 slide MSO would have 10 states. Slides can be any image or graphic. The slides are aligned and stacked on top of each other. While selected, but *not* grouped, they are then converted into an MSO using the Object States panel. Slideshows are usually more effective if their contents have similar orientations and sizes. MSOs can be nested within other MSOs.

Buttons are used to navigate the states in the MSO by targeting the next or previous state. Clicking the buttons in an interactive document would activate the slides, which would not be visible until clicked.

Horizontal Slideshow

Vertical Slideshow

Reset slides

These slideshows have an invisible first state that hides them until activated. Starting one slideshow automatically hides the other one. The Reset button deactivates both states.

Making a Double Slideshow MSO

- Align the slideshow images on top of each other according to their vertical or horizontal orientation. Do **not** group them.
- Select all the vertical images and convert them to a multi-state object by clicking the + in the bottom of in the Object States panel. Name this MSO.

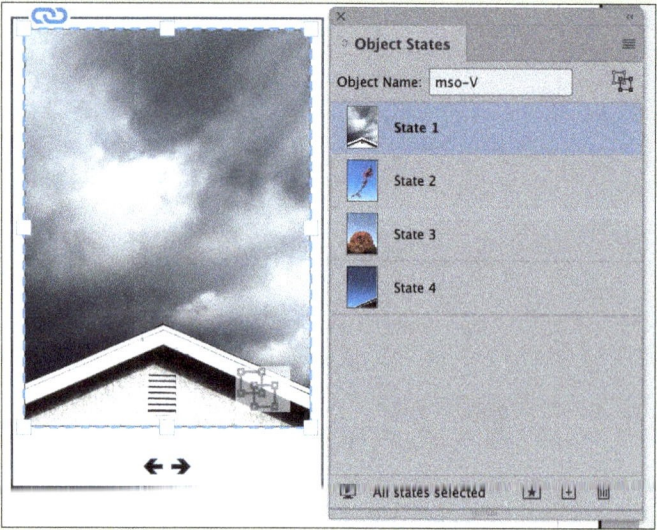

- Make the forward and back buttons (or use ones from the Sample Buttons and Forms panel). Target the buttons (in the Buttons and Forms panel) to the **Next** and **Previous** states of the newly created MSO. Buttons can be programmed to stop at the first/last slide, or cycle through continuously.
- Using a **text frame** with one empty paragraph, make a background for the slide show. Position the MSO in the frame and anchor it to the empty paragraph. Position the buttons—they don't need to be anchored.

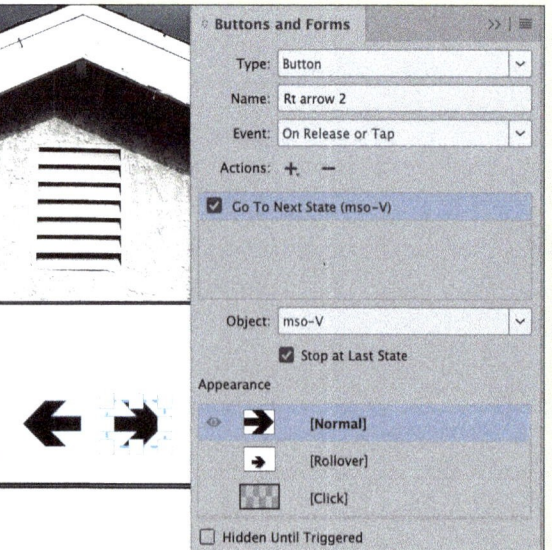

- Group these objects, and convert to an MSO.
- Repeat this procedure to make the horizontal slideshow MSO.
- Stack the two slideshows, plus an empty frame large enough to cover them, and convert to an MSO. Name it for easy identification.
- Make a two-state (active/inactive) MSO "button" for each of the slideshows. An invisible button (unfilled frame) on top of each MSO will target the relevant slideshow state to make it visible. Switch one button's state to inactive, and make the other button's state active.

The images for the slideshow are stacked on top of each other and aligned using the Align panel. While still selected, they are converted to an MSO:

Buttons programmed to go to the *Next* and *Previous* states of the MSO are positioned and grouped with the slideshow MSO:

This group is anchored into an empty paragraph of a text frame that is the background for the slideshow. Note: this step is only necessary if you want to have a custom background for the slideshow. This grouping is converted to an MSO if it is to be nested with other slideshows.

Link to this section online:
https://indd.adobe.com/view/59dcb095-ee0f-4b3d-b153-04ba1fa13d91

(Internet connection required)

Considerations for Digital and Print Output

¶ Initial document setup is usually dependent on the intended outcome: will it be commercially printed on a traditional (offset) or digital (on-demand) press; will it only exist as a digital file? In commercial printing, both traditional and digital printing methods have their own pros and cons. Traditional printing is ideal for larger print runs and can create unique textures and effects, but can be time-consuming and less precise. Digital printing is ideal for short print and on-demand runs, and allows for greater flexibility in design, but may be more expensive for larger print runs. It may not be suitable for certain materials or printing techniques. When choosing a printing method, it's important to consider the needs of the project and the desired outcome.

Starting With Spreads

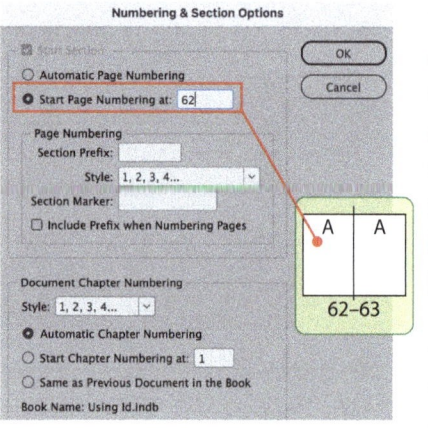

The type of project will determine whether you will be working with spreads or not. Starting with a spread, also known as Facing Pages, is often necessary when working with long documents. For example, to ensure that a section or chapter start is always on a recto/right page, you can use a spread-based template for internal pages. This is particularly useful for books that have multiple contributors. Remember, one sheet of paper is two pages (front and back sides) and so design accordingly: an odd number of pages implies a blank page will be included.

To work in spreads, InDesign needs to begin with an even page number. You can set this up with a section start, either found under the Layout menu (Layout > Numbering & Section Options) or by right-clicking the page number in the Pages panel, choosing Numbering & Section Options, and setting your start page to an even number. You may need to select Allow Document Pages To Shuffle from the Pages panel pull-down menu if you are going to reorder (shuffle) pages from within the panel. To export the side-by-side pages to PDF as spreads, click the Spreads button (in the Pages section of the export dialog panel).

Color Spaces, Graphic Formats and Resolution

You should assume that all output will be to press, and that your color space for graphics is CMYK (grayscale and spot colors are part of this category). While InDesign can import RGB and many other file formats, color shifts will occur if you have not changed the color spaces for graphics prior to importing them (usually done in Photoshop). PDF creation does allow for in-workflow conversions from RGB to CMYK (this is not a default setting), but doing so does run the risk of color shifting. Colors particularly vulnerable to shifting are the bright blues and greens possible in RGB, but not printable with CMYK inks. Shifting from a CMYK to a RGB color space will not induce a color shift, but going from RGB to CMYK might.

The CMYK color space is named for the color of the separate ink plates used to reproduce the image colors—Cyan, Magenta, Yellow, and Black (referred to as Key so as not to be confused with blue). The color image is separated out into these four component colors, each on its own plate. These plates print on top of one another, mixing to produce the tonalities of the image. It is a *reflected* color model. The printed image is reflected back at you. Theoretically, mixing pure cyan, magenta and yellow should create black. But it doesn't. It produces a muddy gray color since the printing inks are not "pure" enough, and the printing substrates are not reflective enough. Black ink is added to create a deeper, darker hue when the colors are mixed. Rich black is a mix of all the inks and is used to produce a deeper black not attainable with 100% black ink alone. There are 16 thousand color possibilities in CMYK.

Rich Black mixes are dependent on the type of presses used by the printer. A good starting point is a mix value of C60, M40, Y40, K100. RGB values have to be converted to CMYK in order to print. Note that color shifts often occur because the two color spaces are not aligned in a one-to-one configuration. For example, RGB Blue and Green appear more vibrant than in the CMYK space. RGB Black is the equivalent of C75, M68, Y67, K90, not as deep as the rich black value cited earlier. When working in Photoshop its default color space is RGB. To produce files for print without changing the color space, you can simulate or preview the CMYK space to see how the colors may shift. Not all Photoshop filters and blend modes work in CMYK, and some that do produce different results. If you have calibrated your monitor, these shifts may be very apparent. There are 16.7 million color possibilities in RGB.

> Most printers simulate gray by using halftone dots printed on a grid; the grid cells are called halftone cells, and the grid rows are called lines or line screens. Each halftone dot is made up of printer dots. As the halftone cell fills up with printer dots, the halftone dot gets larger, resulting in a darker shade of gray.

> Since RGB Black (C75, M68, Y67, K90) may sometimes appear "thinner" when printed, many service bureaus recommend a deeper Rich Black. A common mix is: C60, M40, Y40, K100

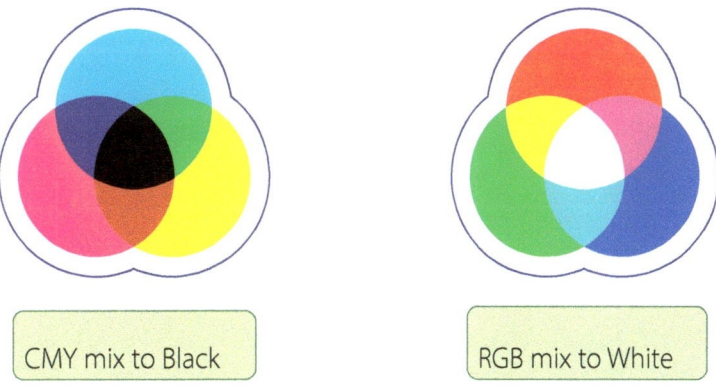

CMY mix to Black   RGB mix to White

In documents intended for CMYK press output, use PSD, TIFF, PDF, or EPS files, preferably uncompressed. JPEG files can also be used. Their resolution should be 300 ppi (180 ppi can be used in a pinch) at the size of their intended use (a 6 inch wide image at 300 ppi scaled down in InDesign to 4 inches wide would have a resolution of 450 ppi). Resolutions higher than 300 ppi do not increase quality, only the printing times involved. For *output to desktop printers* you can use files at much lower resolutions.

Digital documents are usually created using the RGB color model. It is a *projected* color space: you are looking at a screen that projects the image to you. Red, Green and Blue light mix to produce white, while Black is the product of no projection. Non-postscript printers, typical inkjet and laser printers, use the RGB color space. They do not separate colors out to plates, but use dots of color printed in proximity to each other to reproduce the image. Note that while non-postscript printers use ink names that mimic press printing, their colors are different. Non-postscript printer cartridges use dye-based inks, while the inks used on presses are pigment-based.

Process and Spot Colors

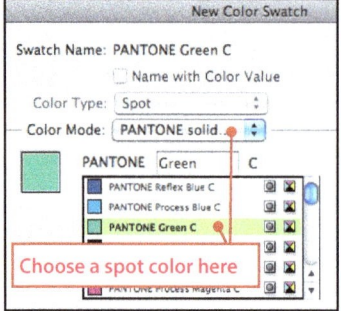

These are the two main ink types used in commercial printing. *Spot colors*, often referred to as *solid* colors, are special premixed inks that are used instead of, and sometimes in addition to, process inks. They require their own printing plates on a printing press. Usually spot colors are used when few colors are specified (usually three or less) and color accuracy is critical. Spot color inks can accurately reproduce colors that cannot be reproduced by process colors, including metallic, fluorescent and varnish finishes. Company logos are often created using spot colors.

Process colors are printed using a combination of the four standard process inks: cyan, magenta, yellow, and key/black (CMYK), and are used when a job requires so many colors that using individual spot inks would be expensive or impractical, as when printing color photographs. *Spot colors* are commonly used with process colors to add a varnish finish, or accent that cannot be achieved with CMYK alone (this results in additional plates being used in printing). Both types of color can be specified in the Swatches panel.

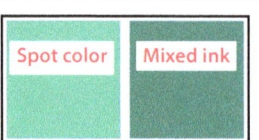

When you need the most number of printed colors from the least number of inks, InDesign also allows for the creation of *Mixed Ink swatches*. These mixed inks are especially useful for extending the tonal palette for two- and three-color jobs. In order to create a mixed ink swatch, you first need to import a spot color (InDesign has many built-in color libraries available). From the pull-down menu on the *Swatches* panel choose New Color Swatch, and then select a spot color (like PANTONE solid) from the *Color Mode* pull-down. Once you've done this, go back to the Swatches panel pull-down and choose New Mixed Ink Swatch (it should no longer be grayed-out). Mix the inks to get the color you want.

About Ink Trapping

When an offset printed document uses more than one ink on the same page, each ink must be printed in register, that is perfectly aligned, with any other inks that it abuts, so that there is no gap where the different inks meet. However, it's impossible to ensure exact registration for every object on every sheet of paper running through a printing press, so misregistration of inks can occur. Misregistration causes an unintended gap between inks. You can compensate for misregistration by slightly expanding one object so that it overlaps an object of a different color—a process known as trapping. By default, placing one ink over another will knock out, or remove, any inks underneath to prevent unwanted color mixing. But trapping requires that inks overprint, or print on top of each other, so that at least a partial overlap is achieved.

Most traps employ *spreading*—expanding a light object into a dark object. Because the darker of two adjacent colors defines the visible edge of the object or text, expanding the lighter color slightly into the darker color maintains the visual edge.

Trapping is less of an issue in 4 color printing since there will always be a common color in the mix— green = c+y, blue = c+m, red = m+y, so blue and red have magenta in common, green and red have yellow in common, and blue and green have cyan in common—and so misregistration is less noticeable, since these colors overprint. Printing with two or more spot colors does require trapping since, they knockout by default, that is, the top color punches a hole in the underlying one in order to maintain its color purity.

Remember:

- Before submitting a job to a service provider, talk to them about their requirements. They usually have valuable guidelines on document setup and submission.
- It is best to leave the trapping values at their InDesign defaults, unless you have spoken to the service provider and they have given you customized settings. Most service providers use specialized trapping and imposition software.
- Full color printing uses 4 plates (C+M+Y+K).
- Using spot colors in addition to process colors will add extra plates to the printing process (and to the cost). Mixed inks do not add extra plates (since they are created from the existing spot colors), neither do tints. Spot colors can also be added for additional effects, such as varnishes, metallic accents etc.
- One, two or three color jobs typically use spot colors (which may be metallic or fluorescent in nature).
- Black is considered a color—clients will often ask for a two-color job, for example dark red and blue, and expect the text to be in black. That is really a three-color job.
- Process colors are semi-transparent, and overprint (hence the use of different screen angles to avoid obvious line-screen patterns.
- Spot colors are semi-opaque, and are referred to as "solid." They knockout by default.

Gradients and Gradient Feather

Gradients are applied as Gradient Swatches, and are created in the Swatches panel. You can use any colors, including mixed inks, in gradients. Use the *Gradient Swatch Tool* to set the angle or direction of the gradient, and the Gradient panel to modify the type of gradient and its ramp. The *Gradient Feather Tool* is used to create a ramp that goes from color to "paper" or transparent (double-clicking the tool will open the Effects panel where you can fine tune it). Strokes can also have gradients applied to them.

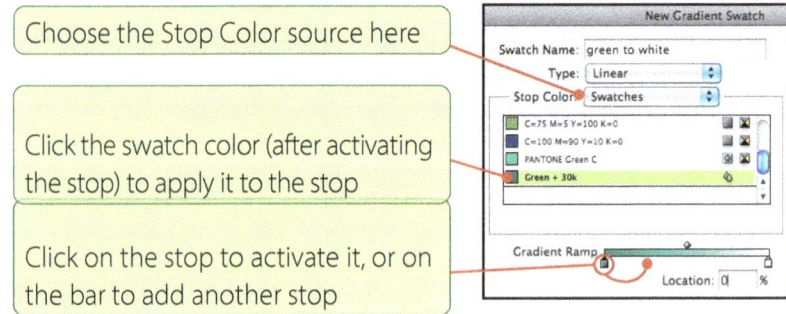

Choose the Stop Color source here

Click the swatch color (after activating the stop) to apply it to the stop

Click on the stop to activate it, or on the bar to add another stop

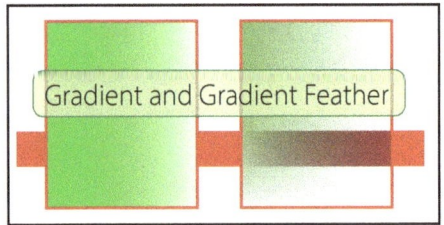

Gradient and Gradient Feather

This adjacent example shows the difference between a gradient (which goes to a solid color) and a gradient feather (which ramps to transparent). To restrict the gradient feather to the fill only (by default, the tool applies it to the "object"), you will need to apply it to the fill attribute only, by clicking the *fx* icon in the Options bar or at the bottom of the Effects panel and choosing Gradient Feather. In that panel you uncheck the settings for "object" and apply them to "stroke".

Adding Color to Grayscale Images

You are able to tint grayscale tiffs or PSDs with any colors available in your swatches. Use any Selection Tool to select the image—when you hover over the focus circles the Selection tool cursor will change to a hand. Double-clicking selecst the image. You can then choose the color you want to use from the Swatches panel (you are essentially swapping black ink with colored ink).

Further effects, like pseudo-duotones, can be achieved by tinting the *frame's* background. Use the Selection Tool to select the frame, and then apply the fill-color from the Swatches panel.

Original image with a yellow (Y100) tint applied to the background

Image selected and a green tint (C100 M30 Y100 K30) applied

Original image

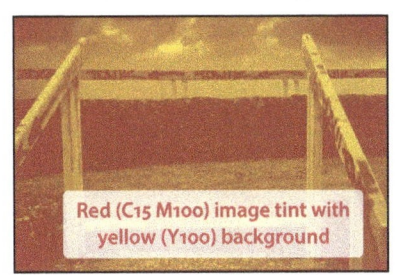
Red (C15 M100) image tint with yellow (Y100) background

Blue (C100 M50) image tint with 45% Cyan background

Single Pages and Spreads

Facing pages, spreads, are the typical setup for documents destined for offset press printing. While the left and right pages can be independent of each other, spreads should be seen as a single entity, rather than two separate ones. However, be aware of *crossovers*, text or images that span the two pages. The gutter can swallow these up due to "pinching" caused by the folded pages after they are bound. The more pages there are, the more pronounced this pinching may be, depending on where they fall in the document. This is particularly noticeable with diagonal text or images. Leave about 18 pts of space away from the center of the gutter to accommodate for the gutter creep or pinch and set your margin guides accordingly. If setting a

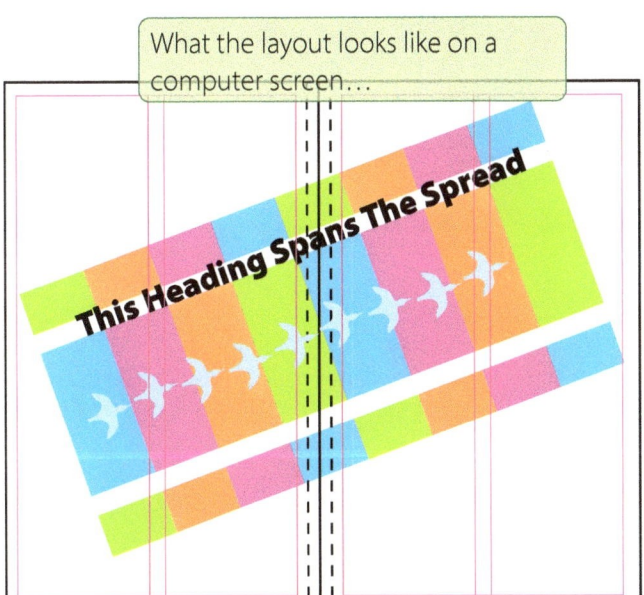
What the layout looks like on a computer screen…

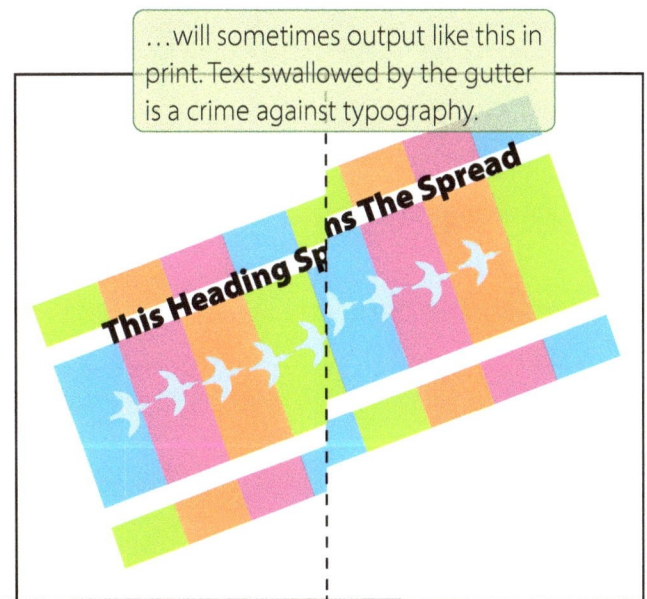
…will sometimes output like this in print. Text swallowed by the gutter is a crime against typography.

headline to span the spread, space the letters falling on the crossover to lessen the effect of the pinch caused by the fold. Consider using two text frames to create the gap between the letters.

Binding will always suck up space across the center gutter in printed documents. Assume that you will always loose at least 18 pts (0.25 in) irregardless of the binding method (perfect, stitched, stapled etc.).

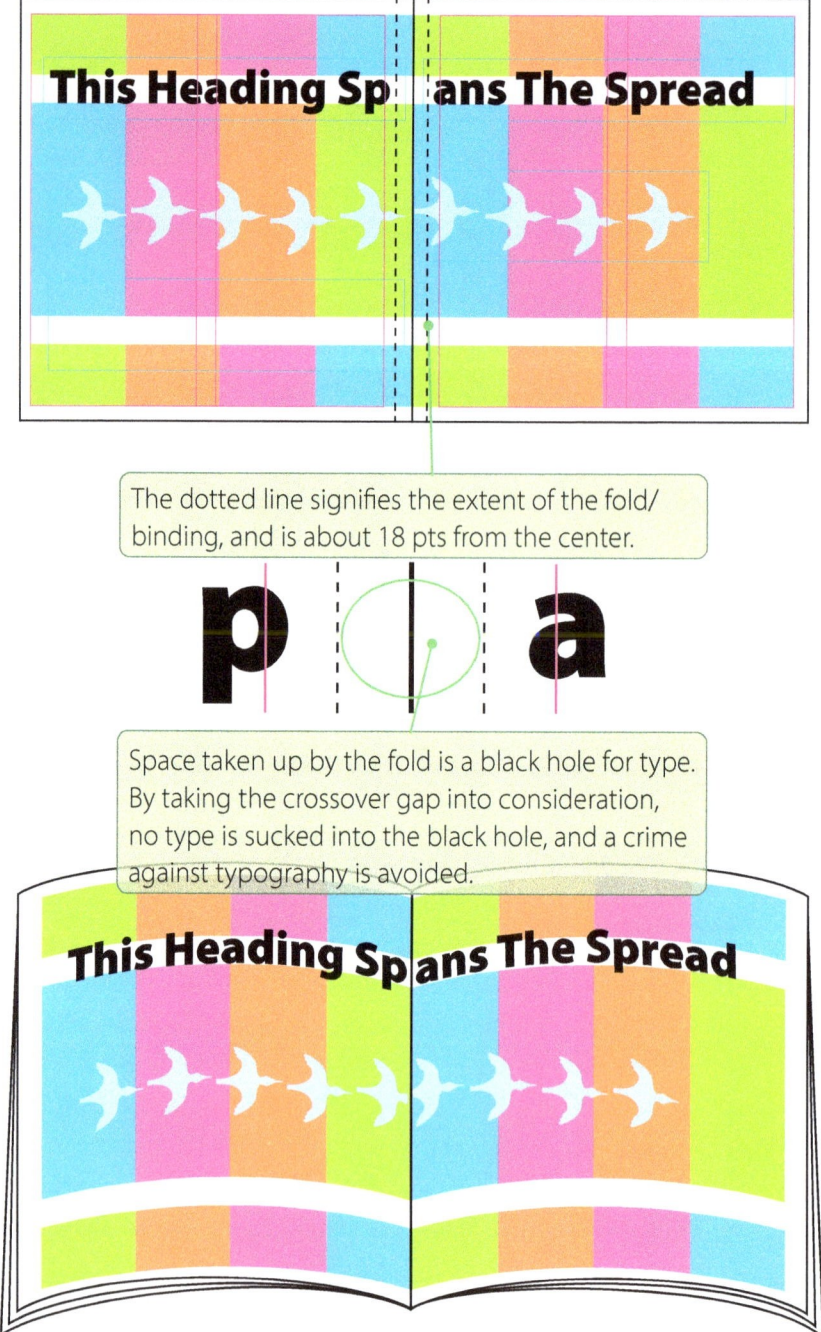

The dotted line signifies the extent of the fold/binding, and is about 18 pts from the center.

Space taken up by the fold is a black hole for type. By taking the crossover gap into consideration, no type is sucked into the black hole, and a crime against typography is avoided.

Note: This issue only exists when multi-page documents are to be printed and bound. Digital files for screen viewing will not have these problems, and typically do not need to be set up as Facing Pages.

Print Booklet and Booklet Types

Print Booklet let's you create *printer spreads* (impositions) for commercial printing, with some restrictions. You can't make a new document based on theses imposed pages, but you can make a PDF. Also, if you have multiple page sizes, you can't impose a document using Print Booklet. Since a booklet always requires pages in multiples of four, InDesign will add blank pages to get the correct page count. If you have blank pages within your document, InDesign will ignore them unless you specify Print Blank Pages in the Print dialog box. You can create three types of booklet. They can be previewed in the Print Booklet panel.

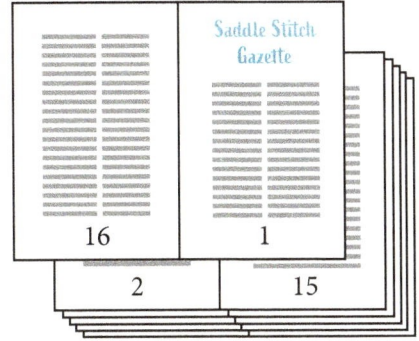

2-up Saddle Stitch: Creates two-page, side-by-side printer spreads. Blank pages will be inserted at the end of the document as needed. Printing is assumed to be double-sided. These spreads can be collated, folded, trimmed and stapled. The Space Between Pages, Bleed Between Pages, and Signature Size options are dimmed when this option is selected. Print Booklet imposes pages based on the Binding setting. If the document has a Right to Left Binding setting, Print Booklet will impose pages accordingly. Choose File > Document Setup to view the document's Binding setting.

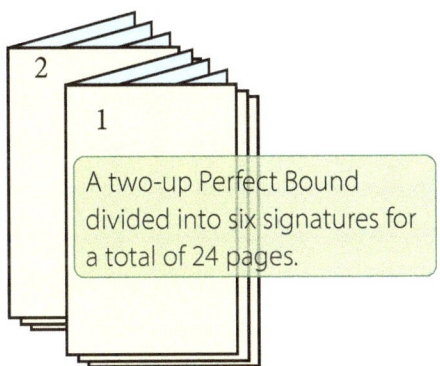

A two-up Perfect Bound divided into six signatures for a total of 24 pages.

2-up Perfect Bound: Creates two-page, side-by-side printer spreads that fit within a specified signature size. These spreads are assumed to print on both sides, and may be cut, bound, and glued to a cover. If the number of pages to be imposed is not evenly divisible by the signature size, InDesign adds blank pages as needed to the back of the finished document. Think of a signature as a folded spread or sheet, and perfect binding as a group of signatures.

Consecutive: Creates a two-, three-, or four-page panel foldout for a booklet or brochure. The Bleed Between Pages, Creep, and Signature Size are dimmed when a Consecutive option is selected. For example, if you want to create printer spreads for a traditional six-panel, trifold brochure, choose 3-up Consecutive. Typically you set up trifolds as one page with three different columns. Using Print Booklet imposition, you can simply create pages that are the size of each panel.

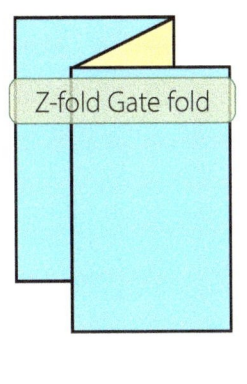
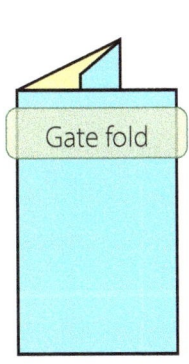

Imposition

The process of converting layout spreads to printer spreads is called imposition. When files are sent to a printing press, they are often printed on larger sheets of paper and laid out, imposed, in an arrangement of the document's pages on the printer's sheet for faster printing, simplified binding and less paper waste. Correct imposition minimizes printing time by maximizing the number of pages per impression, reducing cost of press time and materials. To achieve this, the printed sheet must be filled as fully as possible. InDesign can take care of this using Print Booklet. But sometimes you have to do it manually.

By default, the spreads you see when you choose Facing Pages to set up an InDesign document are *reader (layout) spreads*—they appear onscreen as they would appear in a printed document, in the correct side by side order, and back-of-page to front-of-page order when the pages are turned. This is usual for printing on desktop printers with their standardized paper requirements: one page to one sheet of paper (the backside of the sheet is blank) or two pages to one sheet (both sides of the sheet may be printed).

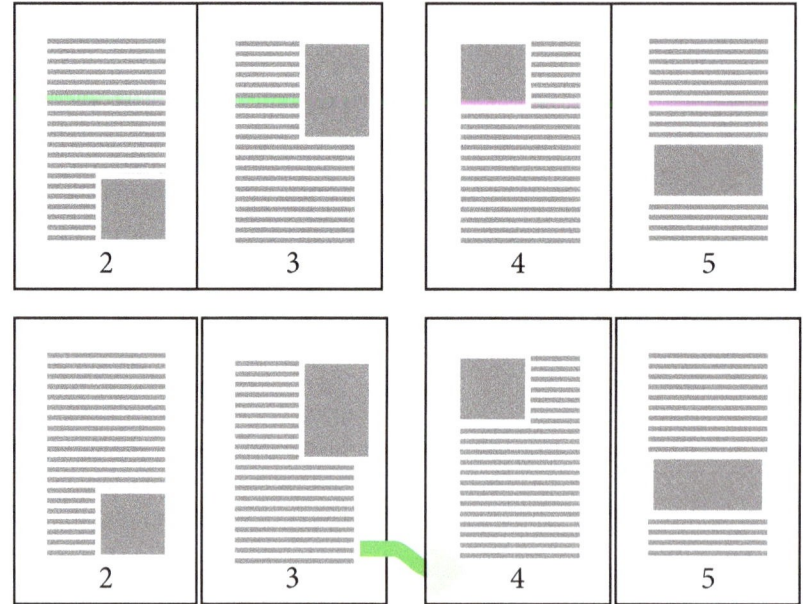

Spreads are displayed side-by-side like this.

Note: Even numbers are always on the left of a spread.

When printed to desktop printers, pages are usually output as one page per sheet. In duplex (double-sided) printing page 3 would be behind page 4, on the same sheet of paper, page 5 behind page 6 and so on.

The simplest and perhaps most common imposition you may need to do is saddle stitched: one spread (two pages) per side, bound by staples in the center. Generally, you set a document up according to the page size you are using and select Facing Pages to create the spread. For a simple imposition, you create a non-facing pages document that is the *spread* size, and the pages are defined by columns which are the equivalent of the pages. Note that for this type of imposition your page count will be in multiples of four (each sheet has two spreads/four pages), and page numbering will have to be done manually to correctly number the pages. The pages that you see side by side in the finished document are not facing each other in the onscreen layout, except for the literal center spread.

This type of imposition is quite common for comics, zines or any type of binding that is stapled in the center of the sheet. Consider a 12 page booklet. This would be set up as a six-page two-column document. It would print on three sheets of paper stacked on top of each other. The total number of pages for this type of imposition should be multiples of four to avoid blank pages (remember, one sheet has four pages). To get the correct pagination, create a mock-up of the number of spreads/facing pages. Since InDesign would regard this as a six-page document, page numbering would have to be done manually. Diagrammatically it would look like this diagram below (even numbers are always on the left and odd numbers on the right), with the numbers zigzagging sequentially across the "spreads."

This is how a 12 page booklet would be set up, with columns as "pages". The InDesign document is set up to match the spread size. For example, two vertical letter-sized facing pages are equivalent to a single horizontal 11x17 page.

The "pages" are created by specifying two columns during set up. Note that the gutter width should be at least twice the outer margin width to accommodate the paper fold.

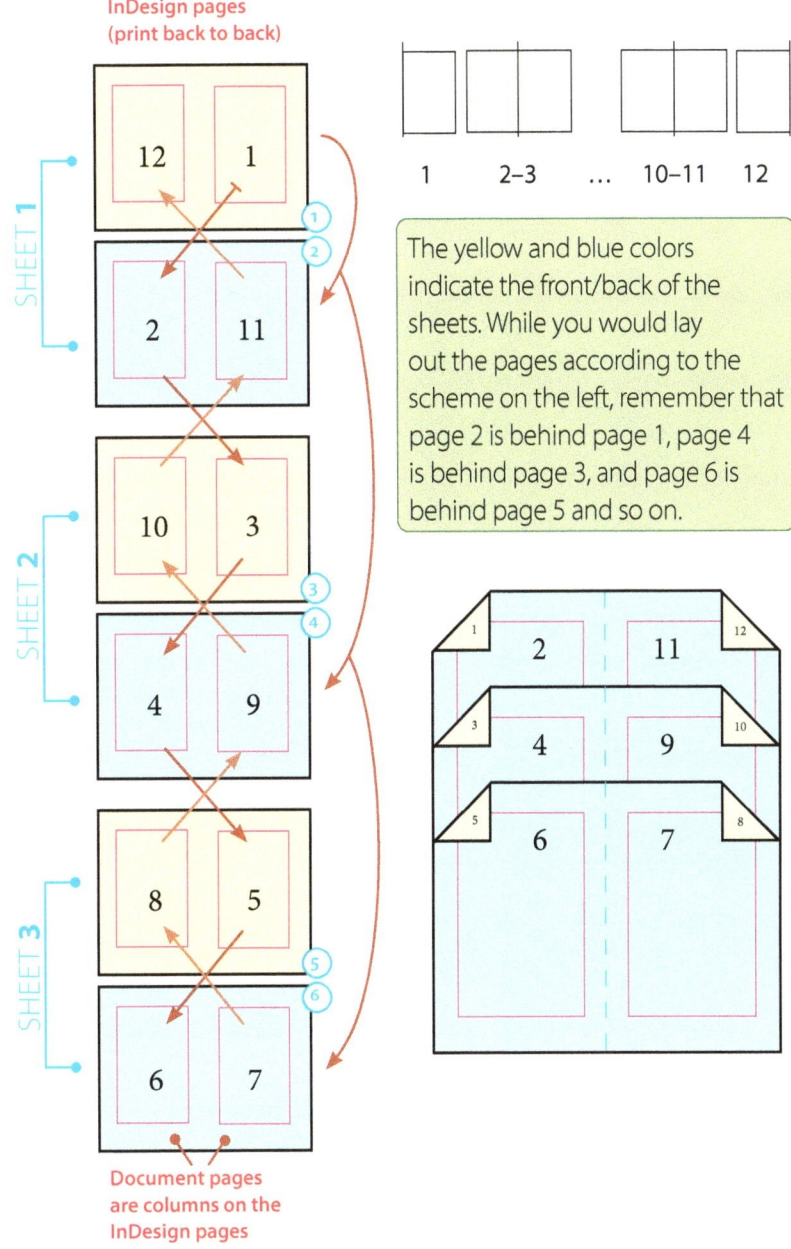

The yellow and blue colors indicate the front/back of the sheets. While you would lay out the pages according to the scheme on the left, remember that page 2 is behind page 1, page 4 is behind page 3, and page 6 is behind page 5 and so on.

Any images spanning across facing pages will have to be manually split and placed on their respective pages. For example, an image spanning pages 4 and 5 would be physically placed on both those pages and cropped to size by its frame.

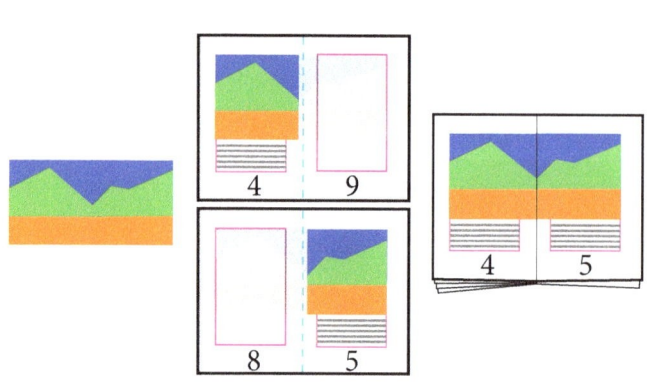

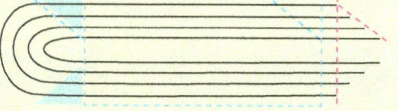

Margins may need some manual adjustment to accommodate the creep caused by the paper fold.

Edge creep (exaggerated in the example) is trimmed. Margins may need manual adjustment to accommodate the creep.

The thickness of the paper and the number of pages influence the *creep*. As more pages are added, the creep caused by the folded paper wrapping around the inside sheets may become quite noticeable on the outer edge of the book, especially with thicker paper stock. This is usually trimmed off in the binding process, so leave enough space in the margins to accommodate this. While not always necessary you may need to manually adjust the page margin positions to keep them aligned within the book.

Unfortunately, such adjustments are tedious. The easiest way of doing this is to group all the elements on the "page" and then use the arrow keys to move them left or right by a few points, or any increment you choose. The outer pages will require more adjustment than those closer to the center. Depending on your layout, the white space around text and images etc., you may not need to make too many of these adjustments.

Why would you worry about this type of layout? Printing costs are high and this method is very cost-effective for low page count short-run jobs on a tight budget. Think about a small elementary or middle school that has never had a yearbook, or and NGO that would benefit from an annual report but assumes they can't afford it. InDesign can sometimes automate this process with its Print Booklet feature (File > Print Booklet…).

Preflighting, Output and Packaging

Before printing or handing off a document to a service provider, you should *preflight* it. The Preflight panel will indicate problems that can prevent a document from printing or outputting correctly. These may include missing files or fonts, low-resolution images, incorrect image formats, overset text, and any number of other conditions you can specify. Live preflighting (on by default) will flag overset text errors as your document is being created—the green circle icon ● at the bottom left of the document window will turn red ●. By default, live preflighting flags overset text. You can create preflight profiles for the conditions you want to flag (like double-spaces, text not using style sheets, empty frames, incorrect color spaces for graphics etc.) in the Preflight panel. Double-clicking the circle icon will open the Preflight panel, where you can create the profiles you want to use, or view the Info section to get basic guidance for fixing the problems that are flagged.

In addition to this preflight checking, you should also delete all unused swatches and styles. Each of these panels (Swatches, Character, Paragraph, and Object) has a Select All Unused option in the pull-down menu to isolate the unused items, which can then be deleted by clicking on the trash icon. Once you are finished with preflighting, you are ready to output the document as a PDF (File > Adobe PDF Presets). These presets allow for a number of delivery options.

- ▶ **High Quality Print** creates PDFs for quality printing on desktop printers. Use this for proofing, and final output not created on offset presses.
- ▶ **PDF/X-1a (2001) and PDF/X 3 (2002)** require all fonts to be embedded, the appropriate marks and bleeds to be specified, and color to appear as CMYK, spot colors, or both.
- ▶ **PDF/X-4 (2008)** is similar to PDF/x 3 and includes support for live transparency and color management. It is optimal for RIP processing, digital printers using the Adobe PDF Print Engine, and any file to be printed by acrobat.
- ▶ **Press Quality** creates PDF files for high-quality print production (for example, for digital printing or for separations to an imagesetter or platesetter), but does not create files that are PDF/X-compliant. Many print providers recommend adding PDF/X compliance.
- ▶ **Smallest File Size** creates PDF files suitable for email distribution or displaying on the web. It converts all colors to sRGB and embeds fonts.

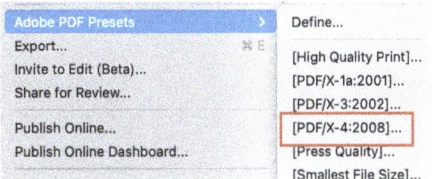

PDF/X standards are defined by the International Organization for Standardization (ISO). If ISO standards are not met when making a PDF you will be flagged with the option to cancel or continue with a non-compliant file. The most widely used standards for a print publishing workflow are PDF/X formats such as PDF/X-1a and PDF/X-4. Before creating a PDF file to send to a print provider, find out what their output requirements are. If your artwork contains transparency, ask your prepress service provider if they want to receive flattened or unflattened PDF files. Flattening should be done as late in the workflow as possible, preferably by the service provider. However, if your service provider wants you to flatten transparency, submit a PDF/X-1a compliant file. You might need to customize the Adobe PDF settings for particular output requirements.

You can also *package* your file. The Package option (File > Package. . .) gathers all the necessary fonts and linked graphics used in the document, and places them in a folder with a copy of the InDesign file. It also performs a preflight check while it does this and will flag any irregularities in the *Package Inventory* dialog box. Packaging is also very convenient for archiving a project and all its related elements.

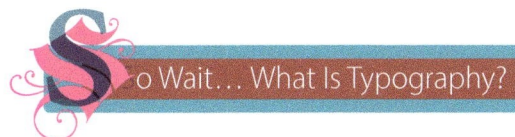

So Wait… What Is Typography?

u•ty•pi•a | yoo-tī-pē-ə | noun
an imagined place or state of things where everything typographic is perfect.

dys•ty•pi•a | dis-tī-pē-ə | noun
a community or society where typography is extremely bad or frightening.

MORE THAN JUST WORDS, IT IS A **combination of letter-forms and spacing designed to convey meaning. It yokes legibility and readability to achieve this.** *Legibility* is its "prettiness"; *readability* is the ease with which the meaning is conveyed. There are as many rules as there are debates about "good" and "bad" typographic practices. And then there is the Department of Typography Police to ensure that crimes against typography are not committed.

Character Anatomy

¶ TYPOGRAPHY HAS ITS OWN SPECIALIZED VOCABULARY DESCRIBING the different parts of the characters. It is these small details in anatomy that separate one type design from another, especially within the same classification: it is easy to see the difference between a serif and a sans serif typeface, but less so between two sans or two serifs. While you don't need to know it, familiarity with this terminology makes it easier to talk about typefaces, their characteristics, underlying structures and differences. And it makes you sound smart…

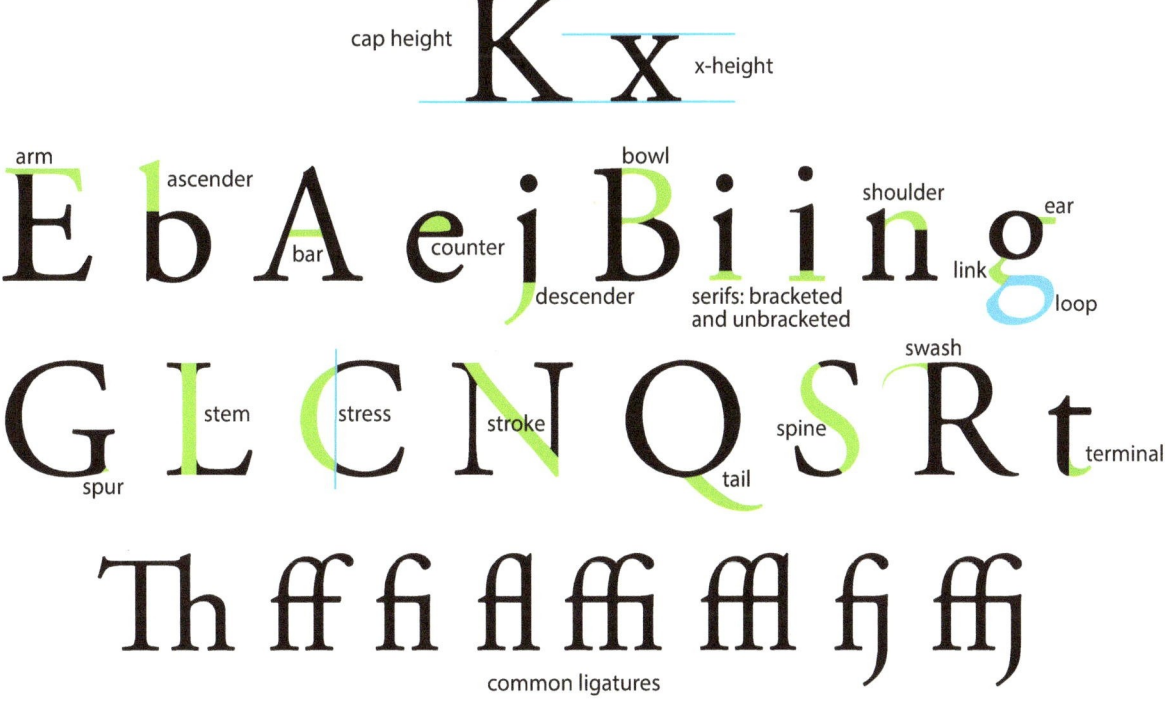

Glossary of Type Anatomy

Arm/leg: An upper or lower (horizontal or diagonal) stroke that is attached on one end and free on the other.
Ascender: The part of a lowercase character (b, d, f, h, k, l, t) that extends above the x-height.
Bar: The horizontal stroke in characters such as A, H, R, e, and f.
Bowl: A curved stroke which creates an enclosed space within a character (the space is then called a counter).
Cap Height: The height of capital letters from the baseline to the top of caps, most accurately measured on a character with a flat bottom (E, H, I, etc.).
Counter: The partially or fully enclosed space within a character.
Descender: The part of a character (g, j, p, q, y, and sometimes J) that descends below the baseline.
Ear: The small stroke that projects from the top of the lowercase g.
Ligature: A special character in a font that combines two or more characters, like "th" or "fi".
Link: The stroke that connects the top and bottom part (bowl and loop) of a two–story lowercase g.
Loop: The lower portion of the lowercase g.
Serif: The projections extending off the main strokes of the characters of serif typefaces. Serifs come in two styles: bracketed and unbracketed. Brackets are the supportive curves which connect the serif to the stroke. Unbracketed serifs are attached sharply, and usually at 90 degree angles.
Shoulder: The curved stroke of the h, m, n.
Spine: The main curved stroke of the S.
Spur: A small projection off a main stroke found on many capital Gs.
Stem: A straight vertical stroke (or the main straight diagonal stroke in a letter which has no verticals).
Stress: The direction of thickening in a curved stroke.
Stroke: A straight or curved line.
Swash: A fancy flourish replacing a terminal or serif.
Tail: The descender of a Q or short diagonal stroke of an R.
Terminal: The end of a stroke not terminated with a serif.
X-height: The height of lowercase letters, specifically the lowercase x, not including ascenders and descenders.

A Very, Very Brief History of Western Type

The core of modern western typography developed over centuries. Its history has been formed by a confluence of assimilations, misunderstandings, accidents and innovation. Its influences stem from Semitic, Phoenician, Greek and Roman scripts. The modern Roman (English) alphabet of 26 letters can be traced back to the 15th century, around the time William Caxton introduced the printing press into England.

Prior to the development of the western movable type printing press by Johannes Gutenberg, books were reproduced from handwritten manuscripts by block printing—words carved into blocks of wood and sometimes metal, a laboriously time-consuming and expensive endeavor. One of the earliest surviving of these books, the *Diamond Sutra*, was printed in China nearly six hundred years before Gutenberg's Bible in the 1450s.

The first movable type press was invented in China in the early eleventh century. It used earthenware characters. Independently, a metal movable type press was developed in Korea in the late 14th century. It is most likely that the complexities of Asian writing systems using thousands of characters hindered the development of mass printing using movable types, unlike the concise alphabetic script of many Western languages: using far fewer characters lends itself to mass production.

Drop caps have their origins in illustrated manuscripts that predated printing presses. First-line indents in printed works resulted from the intentional space left for rubrication (literally, the first letter of a paragraph to be separately hand-stamped in red, and sometimes blue, pigment ink) to indicate a new paragraph. Over time, this practice proved too costly and time consuming to continue, and was dropped. First-line indents, however, endured, and have become the norm in publishing.

Lowercase letters originated in the Middle Ages and were developed from Roman cursive writing. Incidentally, the terms *lowercase* and *uppercase,* first used in the 18th century, were derived from the practice of storing those hand-cut types in drawers stacked below the printing press.

Printing spread from Mainz in Germany (1455) to Subiaco in Italy (1465) to Paris in France (1470) to Westminster in England (1476). It then bloomed throughout Europe resulting in over one thousand presses by 1500. Extant copies of western books printed before 1501 are referred to as *incunabula*. That date is arbitrary since there was no special development in printing technology, other than an exponential increase in the number of presses in the early sixteenth century. Printing was revolutionary, enabling the spread of knowledge and literacy faster and more widespread than ever before.

Western Type has six broad classifications with a number of often overlapping sub categories. These are Script (although types emulating historical flowing cursive writing styles were only produced in the twentieth century), Serif, Sans Serif, Slab Serif, Monospaced (fonts whose characters occupy the same amount of horizontal space) and Hand (fonts resembling hand-lettering). Sub categories include descriptors like Cursive, Brush Pen, Funky, Art Deco, Geometric, Rounded, Western, Futuristic, Grunge and other tags that can apply to more than one classification.

Gutenberg, the Bible, and the Deal with the Devil

While Gutenberg had developed the movable type printing press which printed the first Bible, he was not the publisher. That distinction goes to Johannes Fust, a creditor who lent Gutenberg the money to print it, only to take him to court for non-payment before the printing was completed. Gutenberg lost the case, and forfeited the partially printed Bibles. Printing was completed by Fust's son-in-law, Peter Schoeffer, who was incidentally Gutenberg's shop manager. Typography Police[1] archives suggest that this event formed the legend that became the basis of Goethe's *Faust*, the tragedy of a man who sold his soul to the devil, for knowledge, wealth, and earthly delights. Fust and Schoeffer were the first to introduce printer's marks, an insignia used as a trademark. Perhaps the most famous of printer's marks is that of the Aldine Press (Aldus Manutius), a dolphin intertwined with an anchor.

Oldstyle (1450–1700), Transitional, and Modern Types (1700–1820)

THE FIRST PRINTED BOOKS IN THE WEST copied both the letter-forms and the book design of the manuscripts of the time—Guttenberg's Bible was based on German Textura writing. With the development of Roman types, "scholar printers" such as Nicholas Jenson, Aldus Manutius, and Robert Granjon, who were also publishers, editors, type designers, type founders, and compositors wanted to have total creative control over the printing process. Considered to be among the epitome of Oldstyle type masters, they also produced typography manuals, flamboyant showcases of their styles and notions of typographic theory. These were inspired by the writing manuals created by the prominent calligraphers of the time.

Printed text mimicked hand script, and pages were illuminated by hand, with drop capitals and ornamental frames applied after the printing. The pages were printed from woodcuts and, eventually, engraved plates that allowed for more elaborate and ornamental designs. Calligraphy and type design continued to influence each other over the next two centuries. Garaldes, influenced by Claude Garamond's and Jean Jannon's types, have persisted and are still favored in publishing today.

By the 18th century it was no longer necessary to cast one's own type to become a printer. The typefaces of this period show the evolution away from Humanist styles like the Garaldes (derived from the broad pen) to the Transitional and Rational (pointed pen) types of Baskerville that evolved into the Modern types of Bodoni and Didot. Wooden hand presses dominated printing until overtaken by the precision that eventually came with metal and mechanical presses.

---

1 The precursor to the Department of Typography Police, the *Malleus Typograficarum* or Hammer of Typography, is believed to have formed around 1486 by a group of anonymous scholar printers who felt duty-bound to protect typography from harm.

The Journey To Independent Publishing and the Digital Age

IN THE 1800S THE INDUSTRIAL REVOLUTION LED to technological advances affecting paper making, typefounding, typesetting and printing. This resulted in cheaper and more plentiful books, new forms of advertising to meet the demands of expanding commerce, and bursts of color and special effects that were previously impossible or too costly to produce. Sans serif type was invented in the early part of the century. Slab serif types and all manner of experimental wood types with exotic names Like *Tuscan* and *Algerian* were also derived.

Towards the end of the 19th century Western design saw a clash of movements. Some, like Art Nouveau, Jugendstil, and Arts and Crafts (epitomized by William Morris and his Golden Type), sought a return to the handcrafts of the past. Others wanting to create entirely new modes of production, found inspiration in the flowing forms of nature, while also embracing the sleek geometry of machines, like Art Deco. These ideals were visually expressed in the typography of the time.

The early 20th century gave rise to the "isms" of art, exemplified in design by Futurism, Dadaism, Surrealism, and Constructivism. In the forefront Bauhaus and the New Typography movement modernized typography for the machine age. Avant-garde typographers rejected classical book design and its traditional forms as they sought to find new means of visual expression, while challenging and extending what was considered good typography. The culmination of mid-century Modernism found expression in The International Type or *Swiss* Style, and the love-it-or-hate-it typeface Helvetica.

Beginning in the second half of the 20th century phototypesetting, transfer lettering (Letraset), and the IBM Selectric were relatively affordable technologies that allowed for small run independent publishing that wasn't feasible with other technologies like letterpress or lithography. In 1984 desktop publishing became a reality with the advent of computer technology and laser printers. The shift from analog to current digital printing technologies also coincided with the rise of post-Modernism, paving the way for Deconstructionist design experimentation like Grunge typography.

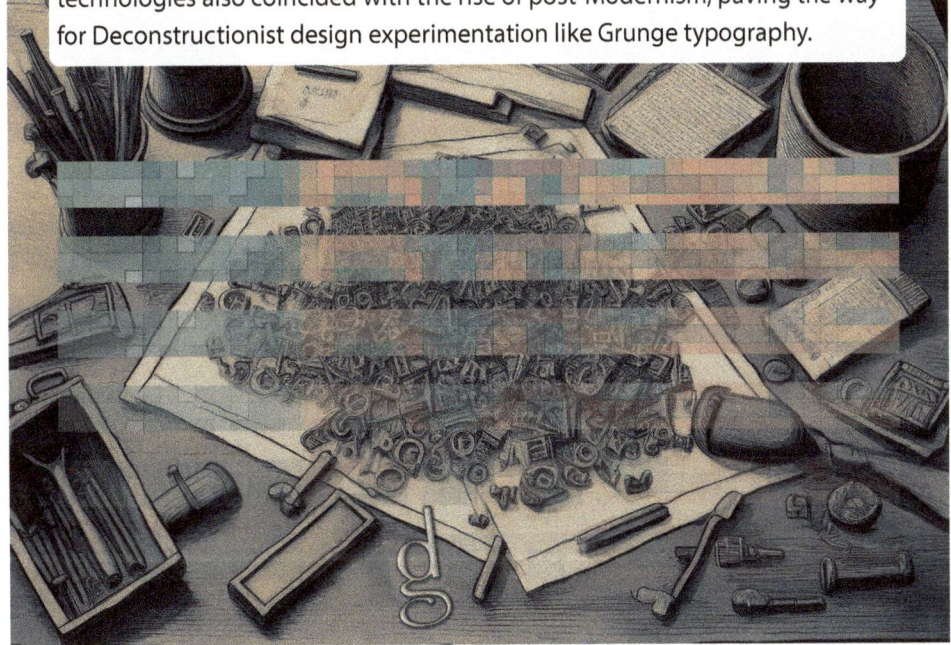

Gutenberg's Bible, from the early 1450s, was the first book printed in the West. It used script types that were based on the Germanic *Textura* or *Blackletter* handwriting of the time.

> **Blackletter** type, based on Germanic handwriting, was the first type used for printing by Johannes Gutenberg in the 1450s.

The first *Roman* types, recognizable by their serifs (lines finishing the main strokes of a letter), were developed around 1465 by Sweinheim and Pannertz. Based on the carved letterforms of ancient Roman inscriptions, these Roman types formed the foundation of *Oldstyle* types.

The finest examples of early Roman Oldstyle types were created by Nicholas Jenson in 1470. Jenson's types were the first to be created using deliberately constructed typographic principles rather than manuscript models.

> Nicholas Jenson's **Oldstyle** types were the first constructed proportional typefaces.

Typography

Italics were invented by Aldus Manutius and Francesco Griffo in 1501. They are based on the handwriting of the time. Italics allowed for more words to be fitted on a page, resulting in more compact books.

> **Italics** applied typographic principles to replicate handwriting.

Typography

The most persistent of Oldstyle types, often referred to referred to as *garaldes*, were created in France by Claude Garamond in 1495. Later types by Jean Jannon (from the early 1700s) were misattributed to Garamond by the French Imprimerie Royale (Royal Printing Office).

> Garamond's **Oldstyle** type design dominated printing for over 200 years and is still in use today.

Typography

William Caslon's typefaces transformed English type design in the early 1720s, establishing its first national typographic style. Inspired by Dutch Baroque types, they were very popular and were the beginnings of the transition to the "modern" types that followed. Attesting to their popularity, the first printed version of the United States Declaration of Independence, printed by Benjamin Franklin, used Caslon's types.

Caslon types were so popular that "if in doubt, use Caslon" was an all too popular sentiment.

Typography

¶ THE PINNACLE OF TRANSITIONAL TYPES WERE DEVELOPED by John Baskerville, a contemporary of Caslon's, in the early to mid 1700s. His invention of "wove paper", which was considerably smother than the "laid paper" of the time, allowed for sharper printing results on brighter paper. He pioneered a new style of typography using wide margins and leading between each line. Initially his printing was met with outrage since it was thought that its higher contrast and definition would lead to blindness.

Initially, it was thought that reading Baskerville's **Transitional** types would make you blind.

Typography

¶ DIDONE, OR MODERN STYLE TYPES WERE DEVELOPED in the mid to late 1700s by Giambattista Bodoni and Fermin Didot in France. These types are characterized by extreme contrast between thick and thin strokes, the use of hairline serifs and the vertical stress of the letters.

Bodoni and Didot pioneered **Modern** typefaces with extreme stroke contrasts and hairline serifs.

Typography
Typography

Serif typefaces like Oldstyle, Transitional and Modern, are considered to be *Humanist*, while sans serif typefaces are generally seen as *Rational*. What's the difference? Think of rational types as those that are hard-edged and "machined" whereas humanist ones are softer, and "rounded." There are humanist sans typefaces, and rational sans ones too.

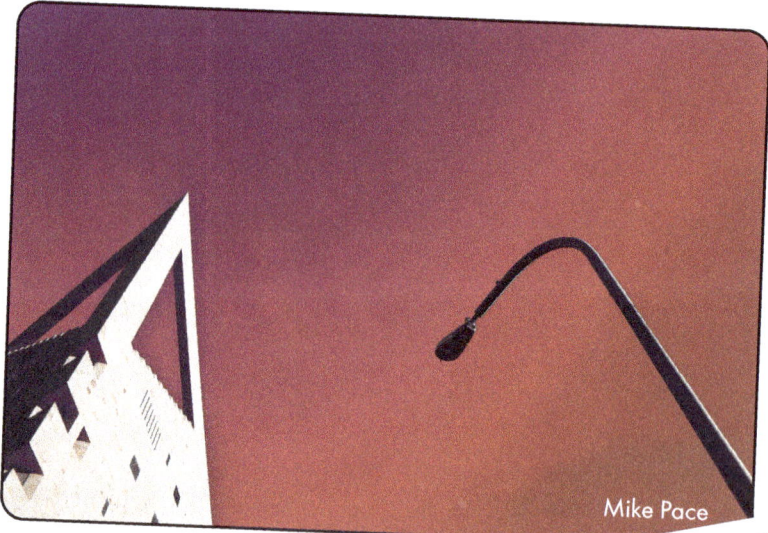

¶ SERIF TYPE, CONSIDERED CLASSICAL, DOMINATED PRINTING FOR about 300 years, until the production of *Sans Serif* type in 1816 by William Caslon IV.

Typography

Printing in **Sans Serif** type was introduced in the early 1800s

The 1800s also saw a surge in typeface design. Slab Serif typefaces (recognizable by thick blocky serifs), often referred to as *Egyptian*, were introduced by English type foundries. They have nothing to do with Egypt.

Typography

Slab Serifs remain popular today.

¶ THE PHILOSOPHY OF *MODERNISM* PERMEATED MUCH OF the early to mid twentieth century typography with its strong emphasis on rationalism. Inherently humanist, serif typefaces were less prone to rationalist strictures that played out in their sans serif counterparts.

Typography
Typography

These two **rational** typefaces have had a lasting influence on typography: Paul Renner's Futura (1927), and Helvetica by Max Medinger and Eduard Hoffman (1957).

¶ *MONOSPACED* FONTS, SOMETIMES CALLED FIXED-WIDTH, FIXED-PITCH, OR non-proportional fonts, are fonts whose characters occupy the same horizontal space as opposed to the spacing of proportional typefaces.

Monospace
Proportional

The difference between monospaced and proportional typefaces is seen here.

Hierarchy in Type

This dropcap is outlined text

A deckhead or lead often starts the beginning of a story. It might be the introductory paragraph, but can be some kind of callout or opening statement. It will usually span the page. It can often begin with a large ornamental dropcap.

Fugia voles quis am, ommo magnam quunt. El et harum es et as quaturem remporundae doles voloru m repedist, soluptatur, niendi rem que alis ius eaquia et qui aut is

Nested styles

exerupta siti sunt, tem ut od que quam ent im rae ducid dusantur aut enecum esed quibusa nduntur?

FUGIA VOLES QUIS AM, ommo magnam quunt. El et harum es et as quaturem remporundae doles volorum repedist, dusantur aut enecum es

soluptatur, niendi rem que alis ius eaquia et qui aut is alit

soluptatur, niendi rem que alis ius eaquia et qui aut is alit rae ducid est exerupta siti sunt, tem ut od que quam ent im dusantur aut enecum esed quibusa nduntur? El et harum es et as quaturem remporundae doles volorum repedist, soluptatur, niendi rem que alis ius eaquia et qui aut is alit rae ducid est ex ut

Callouts are used to break the monotony of big blocks of type, and add interest to a page

---

Guidelines for Hierarchy

Heading can be in a different typeface to the body text, often in bold (a bold condensed sans is used for the heading above)

Subheads
May be based on the heading or the body text. May also be the same size or slightly bigger than the body, usually bold. This subhead is a bold italic sans with a paragraph rule on the baseline
   All the Body text in this example is a serif typeface

Captions (for photos etc.) are often the italicized version of body text. May also use smaller type

Sidebar text may be the same as the body, but is often different so as to not be confused with the body text

---

Hierarchy in Type
A little bit of structure

Heading

Subhead
• Fugia voles quis am, ommo magnam quunt. El et harum es et as quaturem remporundae doles volorum repedist, soluptatur, niendi rem que alis ius eaquia et qui aut is alit rae ducid est exerupta siti sunt, tem ut od que quam ent im dusantur aut enecum esed quibusa nduntur?
Fugia voles quis am, ommo ma quunt.El et harum es et as quaturem rundae doles volorum repedist, so niendi rem que alis ius eaquia et q alit rae ducid est exerupta siti sun que quam ent im dusantur aut en quibusa nduntur?

No indent

Subhead
• Fugia voles quis am, ommo magnam quunt.El et harum es et as quaturem rempo-lorum repedist, soluptatur, niendi rem que alis ius eaquia et qui aut is alit rae ducid est exerupta siti sunt, tem ut od que quam ent im dusantur aut enecum esed quibusa nduntur?

First line indent

This page shows an example of hierarchy: the HEAD is bigger than the SUB, under a sub the opening paragraph can begin with no indent or have a first line indent. No indent is preferred

---

Initial caps don't drop below the baseline as much as drop caps do: they tend to share the same baseline as the first line of type.
   Epel mil inctem que nam eicil magnisti dit am volut moloreperios sam elit lant repre, que provide litat.

Monospaced fonts are typically used on typewriters and for typesetting computer code. They were widely used on early computers and computer terminals which had very limited graphical capabilities.

Monospaced fonts live happily with or without serifs.

Typography

Typography

¶ Decorative, Handmade or Handwritten fonts, including script fonts, are very popular due to their informality and personableness. They encompass an extremely broad range of "cleanliness/messiness" with various levels of distress. However, they do not appeal to everyone.

Sometime you just want to bust out of formality—handmade and decorative fonts work well for this.

Typography

Typography

Typography

Typography

Typography

Typography

¶ There are some that think that type itself should be "transparent" (for humanist typefaces these tend to be the classical garaldes and didones) and even neutral (think rational typefaces like Helvetica or Futura). And then there are those who feel that if they see the word "dog" it should bark at them… loudly.

While some Typography Police favor transparency and neutrality, handmade or decorative fonts are not themselves crimes against typography.

¶

DESIGN GUERILLA Guide to Typography + InDesign | 105

Some Common Crimes Against Typography

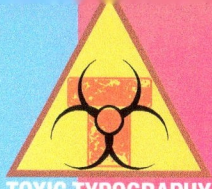

¶ CRIMES AGAINST TYPOGRAPHY OCCUR WHEN TOXIC TYPOGRAPHIC practices are enabled. Even though these might not be willfully perpetrated, ignorance is not an excuse for such cruelty. The Department of Typography Police is everywhere, on the lookout for wanton acts of toxic typography.

Alignment

JACQUES DERRIDA'S THEORY of deconstruction asks how representation inhabits reality. How does the external image of things get inside their internal essence? How does the surface get under the skin? Western culture since Plato has been governed by such oppositions as inside/outside and mind/body.

If writing is but a copy of spoken language, typography is even further removed from the primal source of meaning in the mind of the author. The alphabet represent the sounds of speech with a finite set Derrida used the term grammatology to name the study of writing as a distinctive form of representation.

The intellectual achievements of the West—its science, art, philosophy, literature—have valued one side of these

falsehood. Deconstruction attacks such oppositions by showing how the devalued, negative concept inhabits the valued, positive one.

Consider, for example, the Judeo-Christian concept of the body as an external shell for the inner soul, a construction that elevates the mind as the sacred source of thought and spirit, while denigrating the body as mere mechanics. The original work of art has an authenticity that its copy lacks—the original is endowed with the spirit of its maker, while the copy is mere empty matter.

TOXIC TYPOGRAPHY
Baselines SHOULD align across all columns on a page. But here they do not.

Imperial Measurements

sans
7 " and 7 ' ✗
7 " and 7 ' ✓

serif
7 " and 7 ' ✗
7 " and 7 ' ✓

✗ 5' 7"   ✓ 5' 7"

TOXIC TYPOGRAPHY
Inappropriate use of "smart" (typographers) quotes and "dumb" quotes is a crime against typography. Prime marks should be used for measurements, not quotes.

On a Mac you get: ' from ctrl + ' (quotes key) and " from ctrl + shift + ' (quotes key)

SOME COMMON Crimes Against Typography

Dashes and underlines

There are three types of typographic dashes. If you can't access them from the keyboard (some PCs don't support the keystrokes) you can access them from the Glyphs panel.

-	hyphen
–	en-dash
—	em-dash

Hyphens - [minus] are used to either break words (which is an automatic function of the application which can be switched on or off) or join words to compound their meaning, as in *side-swiped* or *four-legged*.

For numbers use en-dashes – [option + minus]:

626-716-7171 [hyphen = bad]
626–716–7171 [en-dash = good]

Incidentally, in addition to the default (tabular) figure style, you can choose to represent your numbers as *proportional*. Tabular figures have slightly wider kerning values, akin to monospacing, making for good legibility in tables:

1234567890	*proportional lining*
1234567890	*tabular lining*
1234567890	*proportional oldstyle*
1234567890	*tabular oldstyle*

These character attributes can be assigned from the Character panel pull-down menu under OpenType.

An em-dash[1] — [option + shift + minus] is often used in place of brackets ( ) or colons :

El et harum es et as quaturem—rempor undae doles volorum—repedist, soluptatur, niendi remdiset

<u>Underlined text is a throwback to typewriter days when italics weren't available</u>. While underlines may be used, sparingly, for emphasis, *italics are almost always a more elegant solution*. Book titles and literary works should *always* be italicized when referenced in text.

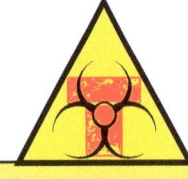

TOXIC TYPOGRAPHY

Incorrect use of dashes and underlines is a crime against typography

---

[1] Apparently AI generated text loves the use of em-dashes…

SOME COMMON Crimes Against Typography

Spacing

Don't double-space the beginning of a sentence after a period. You may have learned to do this, but it is wrong.

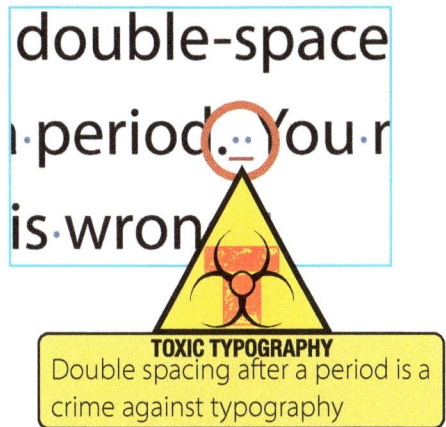

TOXIC TYPOGRAPHY
Double spacing after a period is a crime against typography

Another crime against typography occurs with the use of *justified text*. It is most apparent when the column width is too narrow for the type size being used. Busam estiassitat. Idi sus, se alit optium aborem vitatem porita dolor sumquat uribusa ndaecesed minctora eatem vel idusandae non nianis magnate vendis et es resequatas am inctatusam nos dolut omnis dolupta spidelit quasper iberia nam simillant.

TOXIC TYPOGRAPHY
Justified text can lead to bad word spacing, a crime against typography.

Another crime against typography can occur with the use of *justified text*. It is most apparent when the column width is too narrow for the type size being used. Busam estiassitat. Idi sus, se alit optium aborem vitatem iberia nam simillant.

Bad line spacing caused by auto leading is also a crime against typography, since it sets up inconsistent spacing based on the leading of the **largest** type size within the line in which **it** occurs.

TOXIC TYPOGRAPHY
Auto leading can lead to very unsightly line spacing issues, a crime against typography.

SOME COMMON Crimes Against Typography

Tracking orphans and widows

Orphans have no future;
Widows have no past…

Don't leave *orphans*, those only-words on the last line of a paragraph, hanging around. Find some way to balance the paragraph, usually by changing the tracking values. Do the same for *widows*, those single lines from a paragraph that carry over to a new column.

It's not pretty to see the leftovers of a sentence or paragraph standing all by themselves, so make sure they stay with the rest of the family.

> Don't leave *orphans*, those only-words on the last line of a paragraph, hanging around. Find some way to balance the paragraph, usually by changing the tracking values.¶

TOXIC TYPOGRAPHY
Leaving an orphan is cruel and a crime, against typography

> Don't leave *orphans*, those only-words on the last line of a paragraph, hanging around. Find some way to balance the paragraph, usually by changing the tracking values.¶

> Don't leave *orphans*, those only-words on the last line of a paragraph, hanging around. Find some way to balance the paragraph, usually by changing the tracking values.¶

Tracking the paragraph −20 pulls the orphan up into the paragraph, balancing it.

Tracking the paragraph +20 pushes more words into the offending line, balancing it.

Tracking and kerning values tighten or loosen the text on a page. K e r n i n g affects the spaces between letters, while tracking affects the spaces between words and letters. Use discretion since both are easily abused. What is abuse? For most body text *anything greater than ±60 is probably excessive.* However, intentionally l o o s e l y   k e r n e d   t y p e, known as *Letterspacing*, is an effective design tool if used discreetly. Some fonts, like **𝔟𝔩𝔞𝔠𝔨𝔩𝔢𝔱𝔱𝔢𝔯** or *script* ones, should never be letterspaced. Doing so would be a crime against typography.

It has been said that someone who would callously letterspace these typefaces would probably shag sheep[1]…

---

[1] Attributed to the type designer Frederic Goudy.

SOME COMMON Crimes Against Typography

 𝔗𝔥𝔦𝔰 𝔩𝔢𝔱𝔱𝔢𝔯𝔰𝔭𝔞𝔠𝔦𝔫𝔤 𝔦𝔰 𝔞 𝔠𝔯𝔦𝔪𝔢 𝔞𝔤𝔞𝔦𝔫𝔰𝔱 TYPOGRAPHY AS IS THE USE OF ALL CAPS SCRIPT

Don't leave *orphans*, those only-words on the last line of a paragraph, hanging around. Find some way to balance the paragraph, usually by changing the tracking values. Do the same for *widows*, those single lines from a paragraph that carry over to a new column. ¶

It's cruel to have the leftovers of a sentence or paragraph standing all by themselves, so make sure they stay with the rest of the family. ¶

TOXIC TYPOGRAPHY
Ignoring a widow is cruel, and a crime against typography

Don't leave *orphans*, those only-words on the last line of a paragraph, hanging around. Find some way to balance the paragraph, usually by changing the tracking values. Do the same for *widows*, those single lines from a paragraph that carry over to a new column.

It's cruel to have the leftovers of a sentence or paragraph standing all by themselves, so make sure they stay with the rest of the family. ¶

Tracking the offending paragraph (by –40 for this example) eliminates the widowed line. Using a paragraph style with a Space Before or After also allows the empty line to be ignored at the top of the new column.

 Balance the last line of a column where possible to avoid orphans. The last line of a paragraph should be between ⅓ to ⅔ the width of the column.

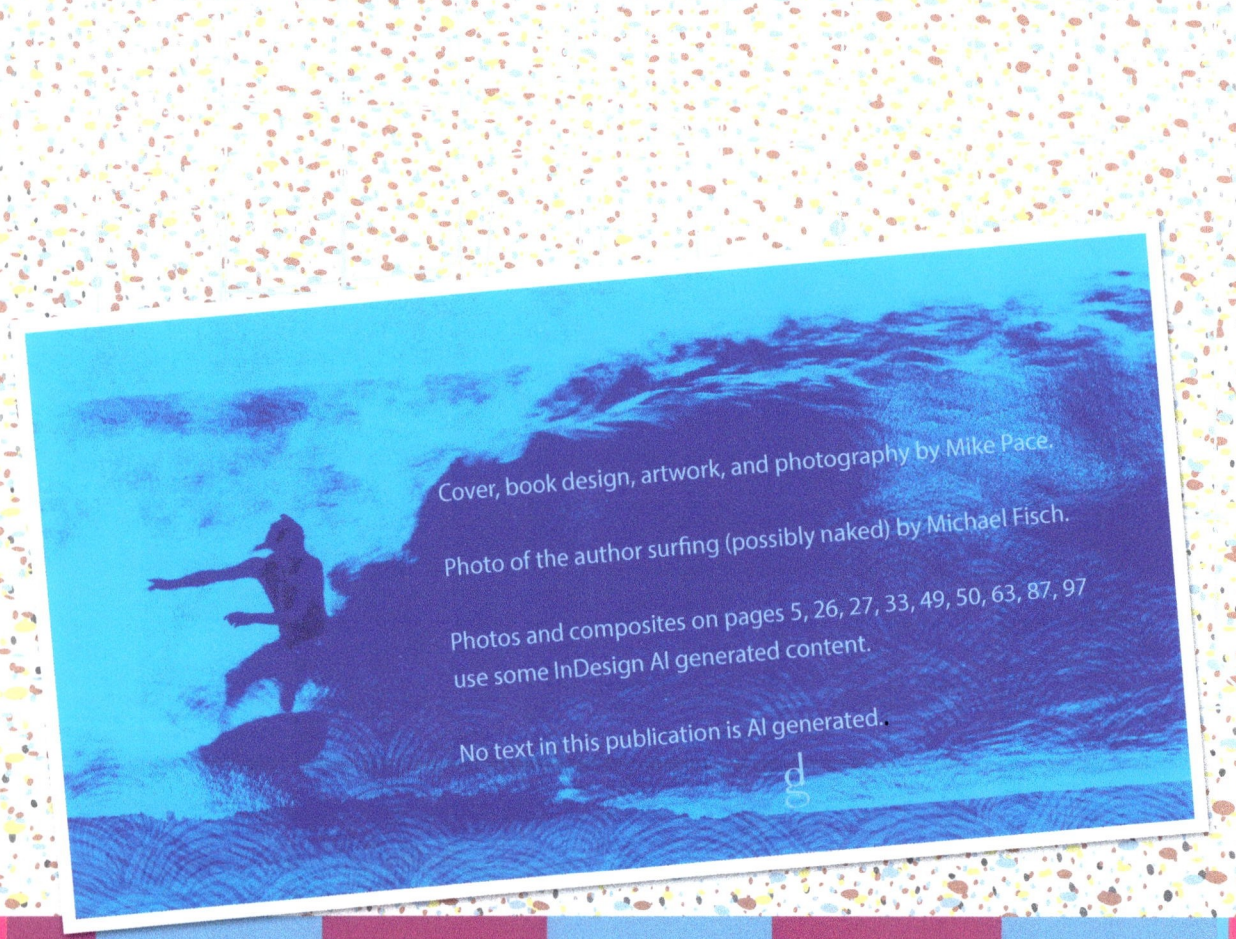

Cover, book design, artwork, and photography by Mike Pace.

Photo of the author surfing (possibly naked) by Michael Fisch.

Photos and composites on pages 5, 26, 27, 33, 49, 50, 63, 87, 97 use some InDesign AI generated content.

No text in this publication is AI generated.

www.ingramcontent.com/pod-product-compliance
Lightning Source LLC
Chambersburg PA
CBHW060935170426
43194CB00026B/2967